KU-059-538

The
Killer Swing

John Daly's Guide
to Long Hitting

John Daly
with John Andrisani

This book is dedicated to my idol Jack Nicklaus
and to Fuzzy Zoeller, my big brother on the Tour

This edition published 1994 for
Golf Monthly Magazine by arrangement with
HarperCollins*Publishers*
77–85 Fulham Palace Road
Hammersmith
London W6 8JB

First published in 1992 by HarperCollins*Publishers*, New York
Published 1993 by Collins Willow
an imprint of HarperCollins*Publishers*, London

© John Daly with John Andrisani 1993

The Author asserts the moral right to be identified as the author
of this work.

All rights reserved. No part of this publication may be reproduced,
stored in a retrieval system, or transmitted, in any form or by any
means, electronic, mechanical, photocopying, recording or otherwise,
without the prior written permission of the publishers.

ISBN 0 583 31736 7

Photographs by Leonard Kamsler
Printed and bound in Great Britain

CONTENTS

INTRODUCTION

Winning the 1991 PGA Championship changed my life in both good and bad ways.

On the positive side, I proved to myself and to my friends and family that I could win a major championship. Consequently, when I raised the tournament trophy over my head, it was my finest moment ever.

I was also very pleased that winning the PGA Championship helped me gain some new fans. I guess they like the fact that I was an underdog who took a big cut at the ball and hit it far down the fairway. And that, on the way to victory, I took time to stop and talk to them or shake their hands. Some athletes turn their backs on autograph seekers. I have never done that and never will.

Most of all, I was happy that all of the hard work I had done in practice had finally paid off. Of course, I had won tournaments before, both on my home turf and abroad, but nothing makes a golfer appreciate the benefit of the work ethic more than winning one of the game's four premier championships.

On the negative side, I learned firsthand that it's true what they say about the price of fame; everybody does want a piece of you. For that reason, I now choose my friends more carefully. More important, I have learned to say no, which must mean that I'm finally maturing and getting my priorities right.

At this point in my life, I work very hard to play professional golf to the highest standard possible. It is also true that when I win, I choose to celebrate in the style of the late "Champagne Tony" Lema, one of golf's past greats. Golf, like life, should be enjoyable. It is my hope to bring new fans to the game and with the help of *The Killer Swing*, this new generation of golfers will hit the ball longer and straighter than any before.

John Daly
Castle Rock, Colorado

1
GETTING READY TO RIP IT

I consider myself a very lucky young man, to be able to make a great living doing what I love most – playing golf against the greatest players in the world, on the greatest courses in the world. The thrill of competition excites me, but what really turns me on is "killing" the ball. In fact, I live for the loud smacking sound I hear when the clubface comes into the ball at high speed and contacts its centre back portion, hard. The next best thing is hearing the oohs and aahs of the gallery as the ball flies out of sight and finally comes to rest 300 yards down the fairway.

For some reason, perhaps because I look big on television, most golfers think I'm built like an American footballer or a heavyweight fighter, and think that's why I'm able to hit the long ball. Well, to be honest with you, I'm very strong and very flexible, but at five-eleven and 175 pounds, I'm no giant. Rather than sheer strength, it's my unique and more natural setup and swing that allow me to hit the golf ball so powerfully and accurately.

While I don't claim that copying my method will enable you to drive the ball like me, I firmly believe that by following my instructions, any golfer can learn to generate more clubhead speed and hit the ball more solidly and accurately than ever before. And when you hit powerful, on-target tee shots, you automatically set yourself up to play a more precise approach into the green and shoot a low score.

Before I review the ins and outs of my swing technique, I want to talk in some detail about the elements of the *setup* that, if you learn them correctly, will make the golf swing itself feel as natural as walking. I'm referring to your grip, your stance and posture, and the aiming procedures of both your body and the clubface. I'll also spend some time talking about the *visualization* process you should develop before taking the club back; I consider this a very important part of your preshot plan.

THE GRIP: AN INDIVIDUAL CHOICE

As you may know if you've played golf for any length of time, there are basically three styles of grip that are popular for the full shots. I'm going to describe each of them to you before explaining my own grip, because I feel that golf is a game in which a degree of individuality is important.   If a grip other than mine makes you feel more secure when holding the club and more confident that you will deliver the clubface squarely into the back of the ball at impact, then by all means use it.

The first and most commonly used style of grip is called the *overlapping* grip. In this style of grip, the hands are wedded together with the little finger of the right hand resting atop, or overlapping, the index and middle fingers of the left hand. The overlapping grip is also often referred to as the Vardon grip after Harry Vardon, the greatest golfer of the turn-of-the-century era, who first popularized it. Today, close to 90 percent of the PGA Tour pros use the overlapping grip.

A second type of hold is called the *ten-finger* or *baseball* grip. In this style, no wedding or overlapping of the hands is involved at all. The right hand simply rests on the club's handle, directly underneath the left, as if you were holding a baseball bat.

The ten-finger grip is employed by a relatively small percentage of professional and amateur golfers. Many golf teachers strongly discourage students from using this grip because they believe that if the hands are not in some way connected, they will tend to work against each other rather than operate as a unit, particularly through the impact zone. Having experimented with the ten-finger grip as a kid, I tend to agree with this line of thought. However, some good golf has definitely been played with this grip. For example, Art Wall, a former Masters champion, and Bob Rosburg, a former PGA champion, both used the ten-finger grip. So I'm not going to criticize it.

The hold that I use is called the *interlocking* grip. To tell you the truth, it was no contest for me which style of grip to use. Ever since I was maybe six years old, I have tried to do everything the way my golfing idol, Jack Nicklaus, does it. And Jack is one of the few of the very top pros who use the interlocking grip (Tom Kite, who is the PGA Tour's all-time leading money winner, is another). While I definitely am prejudiced toward this grip because it's also Jack's, I think it works best for me and may stand you in good stead, too. Let me describe it to you in detail.

The interlocking grip is similar to the overlapping grip in that the little finger of the right hand again is the finger that meshes the right hand with the left. However, instead of the right little finger overlapping the left index finger, it interlocks between the index and middle fingers of the left hand.

The reason I like the interlocking grip is that the two fingers feel more securely intertwined than they do with the overlapping grip. This is particularly important if, like me, you don't have particularly large hands with long fingers.

I think you may have already witnessed how this can work to your advantage on the golf course. Have you ever seen one of your playing partners who uses an overlapping grip make such a poor swing that the clubhead twists at impact, causing him to let go of the handle with his right hand and finish with only his left hand on the club? Well, I find that using an interlocking grip prevents you from losing control of the club, particularly in the impact zone when the club is moving at around 120 miles per hour. Because your right little finger, and with it your entire right hand, is wedded securely to your left hand, your hands will work as a team, thereby enabling you to more consistently deliver the club squarely into the ball. And that is the chief goal of all golfers.

REDEFINING STRONG AND WEAK

Whether you interlock, overlap, or use a ten-finger grip is only a small part of the discussion about how to hold the club. Probably even more important is the way your hands relate to each other, to the handle of the club, and to your clubface and the target.

In golfing terms, for a right-handed player, the more your hands are turned to the right on the grip, the more "strong"

A look at my interlocking grip from three angles clearly shows how intertwining my right- and left-hand fingers gives me a secure hold on the club.

the grip is. The more your hands are turned to the left on the handle, the more you would term it a "weak" grip. A "neutral" grip is one that is in the middle ground between the strong and the weak. For the sake of having a reference point, let me describe this neutral position. First, you would place your left thumb just to the right of the top-centre of the shaft – if you'd consider the top of the shaft a twelve o'clock position, then in the neutral grip your left thumb would be at one o'clock. From there, simply close your left hand around the grip, and you'll find that the back of your left hand faces the target, and the channel or V formed between your left thumb and forefinger points just to the right of your chin. When you now interlock or overlap your right hand with your left, you close your right palm over your left thumb, so that the right-hand alignment matches the left. That is, the palm of the right hand is facing the target, and the channel or V between the thumb and forefinger of the right hand also points just to the right of your chin.

Another method of measuring whether your grip is in a neutral position is to look down at your completed grip and determine how many knuckles of the left hand are visible. If the knuckles of your first and second fingers, but no more, are visible, then the left hand is in a neutral position.

What has been termed a weak position is one in which both hands are turned relatively more to the left on the club handle. Starting again with that left thumb position, instead of it being at one o'clock on the handle, it would be directly on top of the shaft, at twelve o'clock. The V of your left hand would then point straight up at the point of your chin or even toward the left side of your chin. If you were to close your right-hand grip over your left thumb, the V of your right hand would also point toward the left side of your chin. As a final checkpoint to the weak grip, instead of seeing two knuckles on the left hand, you would only see one to one and a half.

Next, let's talk more specifically about the strong grip position. This simply means that no matter whether you interlock or overlap, both hands are turned slightly further to the right on the grip than they would be in the neutral position. For starters, you would place your left thumb a bit more on the right side of the shaft than on top of it, say in the two o'clock position. As you close your hand around the handle, this means that the back of your hand will be facing a bit more upward instead of pointing directly at the target. The V formed between your left thumb and forefinger will point more to the right, toward your right shoulder instead of toward the right side of your chin, as it does when you assume the so-called neutral position. And you will see two and a half to three knuckles on the left hand instead of two. When you fold your right palm over your left thumb, your right palm should again oppose your left palm, so that the two hands match up – the V between your right thumb and forefinger will also point to your right shoulder.

WHY A STRONG GRIP IS OK

If you've studied this game and read a lot of instruction books, you have probably seen a hundred reasons why you must maintain a neutral grip position, with the back of the left hand and the clubface square to the target. The basic thought is that if you start in this position, you're much more likely to finish in this position at impact.

You may also have read or heard through the grapevine that good golfers lean toward the weak grip position, with the hands turned more to the left. The reasoning here seems to go like this: Good golfers are strong golfers, and strong golfers have a tendency to hook the ball. If the hands are turned more to the left, in the weak position, it's harder to move the clubface into a closed position through the impact zone, and therefore harder to put any of the right-to-left spin on the golf ball that makes it draw or hook. On the other side of the coin, most of the prominent theorists say that if your hands are turned too far to the right, in too strong a position, the hands will roll over further through impact, closing the clubface and putting way too much right-to-left spin on the ball. So whatever you do, they urge, don't use too strong a grip. But this is not necessarily true.

All this theory sounds good on paper, but I don't agree with it. Firstly, I think these terms *strong* and *weak* are really misleading and they motivate golfers to think the wrong way. Golfers wind up thinking in "macho" terms instead of in terms of what is needed to hit straight shots. Some golfers, especially the better amateurs, begin to believe that the weak grip represents the good player's badge of courage. If you're a good player, you naturally hook the ball. Only bad players slice it. So you have to use this weak grip to counteract that strong hook shot.

On the other hand, a strong grip position is often considered by many of the swing experts to be a crutch for a bad swing. In other words, the "weak" golfer who naturally slices the ball might have to use a stronger grip to help him turn the clubface back to a square position at impact, and help him hit the ball straight. Well, as you can probably guess by now, I happen to be one of those "weaklings" who uses what is known, technically, as a fairly strong grip position.

Because I travel to courses all over the world to do long-driving exhibitions or play in pro/ams, I see many athletic amateurs struggle to play golf with a weak grip, mostly because they think it is something they *have* to do to be good Owing to this misconception, the typical "weak gripper" starts toying with his swing when his shots fly off line, instead of changing the way he holds the club. Before you know it, he does ten different things wrong. I've seen this happen a thousand times. There are petrol stations all over the country staffed by young men who insisted they could play with a weak grip.

Luckily for me, I didn't fall into this trap. In fact, I realized straightaway, at a very young age, that a weak grip just wouldn't work for me.

Again, I was fortunate in that I had Jack Nicklaus as a model. Not only does Jack use the interlocking grip, but you may have noticed over the years that he places his hands in a position that is just a touch on the strong side. Not quite as strong as my position, but a little bit that way. This helped me as I was building my game and considering one of the many weak grips I was seeing. I said to myself, "The greatest player in golf is one of the most powerful as well, and he doesn't hesitate to use a grip that's a little strong. There's no reason a strong grip won't work for me, too".

I might add that there is a long list of great players who have come to the same conclusion that I have. Foremost among them is Lee Trevino; other current stars with strong grips include Fred Couples and Paul Azinger.

WHY THE STRONG POSITION WORKS WONDERS

We've already talked about the theory that is accepted by most teachers and golfers: At address, the back of the left hand and the

clubface should be square to the target. They claim that from this starting position, it is supposedly easier to duplicate this position at impact.

Although this theory sounds logical, there is one major problem with it. I don't believe that returning the back of the left hand square to the target is a natural position, but rather an unnatural one. Why? Because there is a tremendous amount of stress on the back of the left hand in the impact position when it is directly facing the target. The natural position that your

Turning the left hand into a strong position allows me to deliver the strongest possible blow to the ball.

left hand would like to be in is one in which the back of the left hand is turned slightly upward, with the butt of the hand leading the way through impact. This position is clearly shown in the photograph *(left)*. You can see that the emblem on the back of my glove is facing somewhat upward rather than directly at the target.

Let me give you an image that will help you understand what I'm saying. Suppose you wanted to go up to a door and knock on it very forcefully with your left hand. Would you sweep your arm around and hit the door with the very back of your left hand? No, you wouldn't. Why? Because it would hurt the back of your hand! What you would do instead is bang on the door with the *butt* of your left hand, because that would give it the strongest blow possible.

In golf, too, you naturally want to deliver the strongest blow possible to the ball, and you will do so if the butt of the hand leads the way through impact. I believe that most golfers will naturally want to bring their left hand through impact this way because they instinctively understand what I've just said. I can tell you from my own experience that I've hit thousands of balls using a neutral left-hand grip position, and in addition to pretty weak shots all I got was a very sore and tired back of my left hand. So I said, "Forget this, I'm going back to the left-hand position that's right for me, with the butt of the left hand leading, the left thumb at just about two o'clock on the grip, and the V pointing to the right shoulder."

I'd like to add here that when I place my left thumb on the shaft, I don't extend it as far down as possible but rather inch the thumb up slightly in what is called the "short" thumb position. This minor adjustment feels secure to me and also, I believe, allows me to make a fuller wrist cock at the top of my backswing.

Of course, as you assume this left-hand position, you should be aligning the leading edge of your clubface square to the target.

I've explained the left-hand position in detail because if you position the left hand correctly, the right should follow. Always keep in mind that you want your right palm to match up with your left palm, so that the V between the right thumb and forefinger points to your right shoulder.

A final point regarding my preference for a fairly strong grip position is that I'm not insisting that you place your hands on the club exactly the way I do. Experiment on the practice tee and go with the position that produces the most consistently straight ball flight for you. Quite possibly you may wish to turn your hands a little further to the right on the club handle than I do, or possibly a little less. But I firmly believe that the correct position for the vast majority of golfers is one with the hands turned slightly further to the right than what to date has been considered the neutral position.

GRIP PRESSURE: AN INVISIBLE ENEMY

The position of the hands on the grip has been a basic part of every golf book that's ever been written. Something that's not been covered nearly as often, but which I consider very important, is the amount of pressure you use to grip the club. It's something that's harder to see and measure, because what is heavy grip pressure to one person might feel like a very light grip pressure to another.

While my hands feel very secure on the club handle, I can assure you that I do not squeeze the grip at all. Sam Snead used to say you should grip the club as if you were holding a bird. Actually I think that's overstating the case slightly, but I would say you should grip it with the amount of tension you would have in each hand if you were carrying a loaf of bread: tight enough that you won't drop it, but definitely not so tight that you'll crush it.

If you want to reach your true power potential, you have to grip the club lightly. Holding the club any more tightly than I've just described, will make your forearm muscles tighten up quite a bit; and when that happens, your biceps and your shoulders will have more tension in them, too. There's no doubt that this unnecessary tension will lessen your ability to make the fullest possible backswing turn and generate sufficient clubhead speed to whip the club powerfully into the ball on the downswing.

Try the following experiment on the practice range, preferably with a friend observing. Take your address position with the driver and grip the club as tightly as you can. Then take a practice swing.

Next, reassume your address position, this time holding the club as lightly as possible, with just enough control that it doesn't slip out of your hands. Make a second swing.

Did the two swings feel different? I'm sure they did. And I'm sure your friend will tell you they looked completely different, too. With the tight grip, your backswing was shorter than usual, and as a result the downswing looked forced. With the light grip, on the other hand, your friend will say that the backswing was not only much longer, but it had a smoother flow to it, with a nice easy transition into the downswing.

I know that I am noted for the length of my backswing, which with the driver goes about fifty degrees beyond parallel to the ground. If I were to grip the club really tightly, I could never swing the driver beyond the parallel position. Why do anything that limits your ability to swing the club fully and naturally? Keep that grip pressure light.

A final point I'd like to make about the grip is the position of my right index finger. I call it my *trigger* finger because it is separated from the other three on that hand, and extended down the shaft. This is sort of a personal idiosyncrasy, because it feels as though my trigger finger gives the clubshaft a little bit of extra snap coming through impact. Actually, at the top of the

Setting my right forefinger in a trigger *position allows me to whip the club into the ball at maximum speed.*

backswing my trigger finger comes off the shaft. While I don't do this consciously, I do think that this reapplication of my trigger finger on the downswing adds a touch more speed to the clubhead at impact.

STANCE AND POSTURE: STAY SQUARE AND RELAXED

There should be nothing artificial in your stance or your posture as you set up to the ball for any full shot. You simply want to put yourself in the best possible position to deliver that clubhead squarely into the ball at maximum speed. What I would like to do here is describe how I stand up to the ball on tee shots, then discuss the slight adjustments I make as the clubs get progressively shorter.

With the driver, I advocate a stance that's square or parallel to the target line. That is, a line across your toes should be exactly parallel to a line that is pointing directly toward your target. Picture train tracks, with the right rail pointing directly to the target, and the left rail (the line across your toes) pointing to a spot a fraction to the left of your target.

Even though it seems like a tiny amount of difference, don't fall into the habit of having your toe line aim directly at the target. Although a lot of great golf has been played from this "closed" stance position by champions like Sam Snead and Gary Player, I'd rather see most amateurs stay as square as possible or, if anything, take a stance that's a touch "open" in relation to the target line. We'll get into that in more detail when we talk specifically about the subject of the alignment.

For now, you just want to know that in the driver stance you should get your feet "parallel left" of the target line. Get in the habit of starting your setup routine from a position a few steps behind the ball. As you step up to the ball from there, always set your right foot into position first, placing it along that parallel-left target line. From there, place your left foot parallel to the target line, then spread your right foot back to complete the full width of the stance.

I recommend that you keep your stance an inch or two narrower than shoulder width. Too wide a stance, while it feels powerful, will tend to restrict you from making a nice full pivot with your hips, something I think is crucial to building power. If your legs are spread too wide and stiff, so they look like two-thirds of a tripod, your lower-body action, if any, will be stiff and rigid rather than full and easy. So with the driver, keep the distance between your heels just inside the width of your shoulders.

One small difference between my stance and that of most of my fellow professionals is that both of my feet are splayed out like a duck's, about twenty-five degrees from a position perpendicular to the target line.

Now, most teaching pros say you should turn your left foot out, but that your right foot should remain perpendicular to the target line. The reason this is taught is that when your right foot is perpendicular, it tends to restrict how much hip turn you can make to the right on the backswing. The theory here is that if you restrict the hip turn somewhat, you won't sway your body laterally away from the target on the backswing, which is a fault that causes mishit shots.

The reason I think you should turn your right foot out from the target line is that it *will* allow you to maximize your hip turn. Try it for yourself and see. Take a stance with your right foot perpendicular to the target line, then try to make a hip turn. It may not feel strange because that's probably the way you're used to doing it. Now, take your normal stance and then turn your right foot out twenty-five degrees. Make a nice free backswing. Didn't your hips and midsection turn a little more fully? Great! Keep that right foot "splayed out" so you can make that fuller turn.

You might ask, now that this adjustment allows me to turn more freely on the backswing, won't I do what the teachers of

Setting up with your right foot splayed *outward allows you to make the strongest possible turn.*

the square-right-foot position are afraid of – that is, sway off the ball? We'll talk about the swing in greater detail later, but for now, please accept that as long as you make a nice level hip turn around your spine, you can't possibly turn your hips too far. Turn them as far as you can – after all, why restrict yourself? Adopt one of my mottos, which is, *"The further you turn, the further it will fly."* Then turn out that right foot just slightly, particularly when playing your tee shots.

Your weight distribution should be natural and relaxed at address. Flex your knees just a little bit, so that the weight is centred on your feet for good balance. You should bend just a little from the waist with the driver, but not too much. I really don't like to measure how much you should bend from the waist as some teachers do who say twenty degrees or twenty-five degrees, for example. Just get comfortable. It doesn't take a neurosurgeon to figure out that the longer the club in your hand, the less bend you will need from the waist for your hands to comfortably reach the handle of the club. So you will bend from the waist a touch more with each club as you progress down from the driver to the wedge.

Your arms should hang naturally from your shoulders at address, and really, this factor will automatically determine how far you should stand away from the ball with the driver or with any club. Where your arms and hands hang down to naturally is where your hands should grip the club – this is usually about six to eight inches away from your body. Then the length of the club you're holding determines how far you stand away from the ball. It's really that simple. (Don't fall into the very common habit of stretching your arms out away from you at address. This immediately introduces unwanted tension into the setup and, as I've pointed, out tension inhibits a good turn and square contact.)

One other posture fundamental I recommend is to keep your chin raised just slightly above normal, so that you look down at the ball from the bottom of your eyes, so to speak. This chin-up position will allow your left shoulder to work smoothly underneath the chin as you develop your maximum shoulder turn. If your chin is tucked down so that you look like a turtle at address, it will stop your shoulder turn prematurely. Not only that, but because your chin stops the momentum your shoulder turn has begun to build, you can throw yourself off balance. So keep your chin up.

When addressing the ball, your hands should be about six to eight inches away from your body.

WEIGHT DISTRIBUTION AND BALL POSITION

For the driver as well as the fairway woods, I recommend a weight distribution of fifty-fifty between the feet, which will encourage a shallow sweeping action through the impact zone that is very desirable with the longer clubs. You should feel lively, springy, ready – like a basketball player who is playing defence, waiting for the dribbler to approach and ready to move in either direction.

Your left arm and the clubshaft should form an approximately straight line down to the ball, which should be placed on a line virtually opposite your left heel. This ball position for the tee shot is important because it will allow you to make contact just a fraction after the clubhead has reached its lowest point. Believe me, even I am not strong enough to hit down on the driver and still get the ball to carry a long way. There just isn't enough loft built into a driver to launch the ball high into the air if you hit with a sharp descending blow rather than with a sweeping action. So play the ball almost directly off the left heel and your natural swing arc will actually add a degree or so of loft to the club and allow you to sweep the ball cleanly off its wooden-tee perch.

I tee the ball fairly high for the driver, about one full inch, so that more than half the ball is resting above the crown of the clubhead at address. Again, everything in your setup should encourage a sweeping action with the driver, and teeing the ball high helps you form the right mental picture. Also, with the ball teed up about an inch, you have virtually eliminated the possibility of catching the clubhead on the ground prior to the impact so that the clubface is jarred from its intended line. Play the ball forward in your stance, tee it fairly high, and don't deviate too much from this position no matter what kind of wind or weather you're facing. I've come to understand that if you play around too much with the ball position and tee height, you make it difficult for yourself to keep a nice consistent flow in your driver swing. In the long run, that's far more important than the few yards you might save when hitting into the wind by playing the ball further back, teeing it low, and trying to "punch" the shot. Stick with a consistent positioning and you'll make more consistent swings.

Playing your tee shots off your left heel will promote a sweeping hit.

SETTING UP TO THE SHORTER CLUBS

If you're like the majority of amateurs, you'll need to hit your fairway woods on all of the par fives and quite a few of the par fours on your course. So let's make sure you know how to set up correctly when playing them.

The only difference in the setup to the fairway woods as opposed to the driver is that the ball is not sitting on a tee. You should again play the ball forward in your stance to encourage an upswing hit. Also keep your weight balanced fifty-fifty between the feet to create a nice shallow bottom to your swing. Keep that right toe turned out a little, too, to help you make your strongest possible backswing turn.

One note I'd like to make for all middle and high handicappers is that if you have what would normally be a three-wood shot, but the lie is a little fluffy, play it smart. Take a four- or five-wood instead, and play the shot from exactly the same address position. With a little more loft in hand, you won't have that subconscious (or conscious) worry that you won't get the ball up out of that fluffy lie. Also, because a little grass may get between ball and clubface at impact, you will get a little bit of a "flier" so that the more lofted wood will give you three-wood distance anyway. Awareness of a small point such as this will definitely save you a stroke now and then.

Long irons are the clubs that most amateurs hate. But the two- and three- irons actually have more loft on them than the three- and four-woods. There's no reason you can't hit them well if your setup is correct and you make a good backswing turn.

For the long irons, assume the same address position as two inches behind a line drawn opposite your left heel. By making this adjustment, you'll contact the ball precisely at the bottom of your swing, which is the key to good long iron play. You don't have to hit down on a long iron as you would a wedge – even I would have trouble hitting a high long iron that way! If you just clip those long irons off the grass with contact coming at the very base of your swing arc, you'll see an immediate improvement in your long iron play.

On short iron shots, play the ball back in your stance.

As you move into the middle irons, there are three slight adjustments you must make:

1. Move the ball back about two more inches in your stance.
2. Narrow your stance width slightly, so there are two inches less between your heels than with the driver.
3. Place a touch more weight on your left side at address, so that 60 percent of your weight is now on your left side.

The reason for these minor adjustments is that now that the clubs have more loft, you'd like to strike the ball with a slightly descending blow, taking a small divot just past impact. This descending blow puts added backspin on the ball to help it sit down quickly once it hits the green. And the narrower stance helps you stay centred over the shot, which becomes more of a priority as the clubs increase in loft. Once you make these three small setup adjustments, just trigger the swing as you would normally.

This may sound a little strange to the amateurs out there, but to me, the short irons, from the seven-iron through the full sand wedge, are the hardest clubs to hit very well. Why? Because the key to hitting short irons close to the hole is hitting the ball a perfectly consistent distance, and that's more difficult for me to do than for the less powerful player. You probably love to hit those eight- and nine-irons because they're easier to hit straight, but they still require care. Let's look at the setup adjustments needed to play these shots best.

The most obvious change is that your ball position is now in the centre of your stance – two inches further back than it was for the middle irons. At address, your hands will be well ahead of a line drawn straight down to the ball. Also, your stance has become more narrow, with just eight to ten inches of space between your heels. Your weight distribution should be a little more pronounced to your left side – say, two thirds of your weight on the left foot, one-third on the right. These setup adjustments will guarantee that you strike with a fairly sharp descending blow so that you put plenty of bite on your shots.

There is one other element of the short iron setup that I consider vital: the position of the left foot. My left foot is drawn back from the target line two to three inches. There is a good reason for this "open" position that many golfers don't understand. You see, with the ball back in the centre of the stance, the clubface is not only striking a descending blow, but because it has not quite reached the bottom of its arc at the instant of impact, it also has not quite squared itself up to the target line. That is, it will be slightly open or pointing to the right of the target line. By opening your stance so you're aiming slightly left of the flag, you'll deliver the blade of the short irons precisely at the target at impact.

AIM YOURSELF AS WELL AS THE CLUBFACE

Even though my heart and soul are into blasting the ball, the name of the game on the PGA Tour is scoring. Of course, you can learn to hit the ball further if you can increase your clubhead speed, but if you don't hit it squarely, more clubhead speed won't do you any good – in terms of direction. There's no substitute for hitting the ball squarely if you want to hit it further and accurately enough to put a big dent in your scores. So you have to learn not only to aim the clubhead properly, but also to aim yourself properly.

The most important element in your full-shot setup is to align your shoulders square to your target line. The reason this is so important is that in the natural golf swing, you will tend to swing the club through impact along a line that is parallel to your shoulder line. If your shoulder line is square to your target line at address, it then becomes much easier to swing the clubhead along the target line through impact.

We've already talked about how to step up to the shot from behind the ball and then assume your stance. Once you've done so, you must be sure that your shoulders are precisely parallel to an imaginary line drawn from the ball to your target. Many golfers have the false impression that if their feet are square to the target line, their lineup is automatically correct. But your feet can be square while your shoulders are either open or closed to the target. If this is the case for you and your setup and ball position are correct, you'll have to make some kind of in-swing manipulation to swing down the line through impact. That's where a lot of swing problems start.

The best thing you can do is periodically have a friend place a clubshaft across your shoulders as you address the ball on the practice tee. Then step back from the ball while he or she holds the club steady, and see for yourself where your shoulder line is pointing. You might be in for a surprise. I know that many times when my shots were becoming erratic, I'd use this simple check and find out my shoulders were way out of alignment. Now I've become much more aware of this critical setup factor and stay pretty close to square most of the time, but I still have my teacher, Rick Ross, check my shoulder line. Do the same and you'll save yourself a lot of swing headaches.

Of course, you have to aim the clubface properly as well. Having grown up with the desire to copy the setup and swing methods of Jack Nicklaus, I do as he does when aiming the clubface. As I step up to the shot, placing my right foot into position first, I simultaneously position the clubhead behind the ball. Then I make sure to line up the leading edge of the clubface with any noticeable object that is right on the target line and a few feet in front of the ball, such as a leaf or a discoloured bit of grass. Make sure that as you line up the clubface with the target line, you do it with the leading edge of the club, rather than the top edge. Because there is loft on the clubface, the top edge can give you a distorted view of where the club is really pointing.

There is one other somewhat individual adjustment I make as I place the clubhead behind the ball which might be helpful to you, too. As I carefully place the clubhead square to the target line, I also address the ball a little bit toward the heel of the club – say, one inch inside the centre of the clubface. This is a little idiosyncrasy that is actually quite common among players on the PGA Tour. In fact, Fuzzy Zoeller actually pushes the entire driver head beyond or outside the ball just before he draws the club back. I don't recommend that extreme, but there is a reason I do address the ball toward the heel. As we'll see in later chapters, my hip turn on the downswing is very active, with a big "clearing" move through the impact zone. Because this turn of the hip to the left is so pronounced, my hands are pulled a touch to the inside of the position they were in at address. Because I started with the heel of the club behind the ball, I actually return the centre or 'sweet spot" of the clubface to the ball at impact.

This is an adjustment that I learned more or less by intuition as I was developing my game in my teens. As I said, it's fairly common on the PGA Tour and I think it's because most of the pros have such a good hip pivot on the downswing. You may not need this clubface adjustment at address right now. However, if you start developing a super hip turn as I hope you will after reading this book, you may notice your hands getting whipped through the ball a little more inside their original address position. If so, just make the adjustment.

WHY VISUALIZATION IS CRUCIAL

So far, you've done everything right and have put yourself in a position to give the ball a real belt. You've developed a nice, comfortably correct address position and you're holding the club with a nice light grip. It's just about time to pull the trigger – but before you do, I want to tell you about the part of the preshot routine that I personally feel is the most important of all. That is the process of visualizing the shot that you intend to hit.

I'd like to tell you something that may sound slightly ironic, because you're reading this instruction from John Daly, PGA champ and super-long hitter. I believe that the very best thing I do – better than my setup, better than my backswing turn, better than my downswing turn – is to visualize a perfect shot in my mind every time I step up to the ball. I absolutely never let a negative image creep into my head either before or during the swing. That may sound simple. You may be saying to yourself, "Yes, I always try to think positively," but I doubt that many golfers truly do the kind of visualizing I do, that's just so positive it almost forces you to hit a good shot. So I'd like to talk to you a bit about visualization.

First, let's look at the positive aspects of playing a golf course. Every golf hole has a fairway and every golf hole has a green and a cup. Those are the places you must determine you're going to be. Yes, some fairways are wider than others and some greens are bigger than others, too. But you need to focus on the fairway from the tee, and on the green and the cup from the fairway – and not on anything else.

Have you ever played a different course with someone who knew that course better than you did, who was telling you about every single problem there might be on a given hole? He might say to you, "Now, on this hole, whatever you do, don't hit it to the right – there's a pond just over that hill and you can't see it, and also the wind's blowing to the right so there's even more chance of hitting the ball in the water hazard." You say, "Okay, thanks," and tee up your ball. Before you get a chance to draw it back, this guy says, "Also, make sure you don't hit it in one of those fairway bunkers on the left. They're so deep it's totally unfair. Yesterday I got a bad bounce into one of 'em, then I buried my second shot under the lip and wound up making an eight." By now you're just hoping this guy will quiet down and let you hit your shot. After all, how are you going to belt it down the middle of the fairway when someone puts that kind of negative thinking into your head?

The irony is, most amateurs have these negative thoughts in their own heads: they do a psych job on themselves! The typical club-level golfer is so concerned about where not to hit the ball that he lacks the mental energy to focus on where he should hit it. You've just got to take the opposite approach, where you see in your mind only good shots landing where you want them to land, on the fairway, on the green, in the hole.

Let me give you a great example of how valuable positive visualization can be; then we'll talk about what you do specifically over the ball. When I went to the PGA Championship in August 1991, I was the last player to get into the tournament. Actually, I was the ninth choice, but because of several injuries, illnesses, and I think one or two childbirths, there were enough withdrawals that I got the call the day before the tournament started. Talk about the hand of fate! Anyway, I drove seven hours from Memphis, Tennessee, to Carmel, Indiana, and showed up for my first round at Pete Dye's Crooked Stick GC, without having ever seen the course.

Now, most people would have said to me, "You've got no chance to play well: you won't even know where the trouble is and you won't know the yardages." Well, I purchased a little booklet that gave me the yardages, so that was no problem. But I didn't know where the trouble was. And do you know what? I didn't want to know. All I wanted was a good look at the fairways and greens, because that's where I believed I was going to put every shot. Frankly, I was delighted with what I saw on my first view of Crooked Stick because it was a big golf course, with pretty wide fairways and big greens compared to many that we see on the PGA Tour.

Meanwhile, I believe that all the guys who came in and scouted the course for three or four days ended up at a big disadvantage. Everybody started talking about how long the course was (7,289 yards) and the fact that it would play even longer because there had been a lot of rain. I think Jack Nicklaus was quoted as saying it was the hardest tournament course he'd ever seen. Throw in the fact that the course was designed by Pete Dye, who is notorious in tour circles for taking pride in "roughing up" the pros, and I'm sure half the field was psyched out before they started playing.

So what happened? Dumb John Daly just kept looking at those fairways and greens and shot a three-under-par 69, playing the course "blind". Then I shot a 67 the second day and was in the lead. On the weekend a really great thing happened – nobody caught me.

The point I'm trying to make here is that without a really positive focus all week long, I would never have become the PGA champion. You must have positive visualization not only at the beginning of your weekend match when everybody is loose and friendly, but down the stretch, too, when suddenly those little bets and presses have added up and they're all going to be determined on the last hole.

It was the same for me on the seventy-second hole of the PGA. I had a three-shot lead, but there's a huge lake all the way down the right side of this monster par four. One little mistake, a slight block or slice to the right, could spell a quick double bogey. If Bruce Lietzke, walking up to the eighteenth green in front of me, should happen to birdie the hole, the tables could be turned mighty quickly.

That's why most of the gallery was stunned when I whipped out the driver instead of playing safe with a long iron. They thought I was crazy. But I said to myself, "I've hit this fairway three days in a row. There's plenty of room out there, so I'm just going to knock it on the fairway again." I went through my normal visualization process, gripped it, and ripped it. When I saw that pretty little golf ball heading down the fairway just like I had planned, I knew I had the PGA Championship won.

THE VISUALIZATION PROCESS AND
THE FOUR Fs

Let's go back now to that point in your preshot preparation where you've stepped up to the shot, set yourself square, and placed the clubhead behind the ball pointing directly down the target line. My visualization process really picks up during the five seconds or so before I start the backswing. Let me explain it to you so you can start using it yourself.

Once I'm over the ball, I think only in terms of target. I've already established my short target, just a few feet ahead of the ball, to which I've aligned the leading edge of the clubface. At this point, if I'm hitting the driver, I focus in on my long target. This is an area of the fairway where I want my ball to land that's far in the distance – maybe 300 yards away, even further than I usually drive it. From the moment I take this look until the instant I draw the club back, all I'm doing is visualizing the long, high flight of my ball to that distant target. All I see is that target area. In my mind I never see the hazards that may be at the sides of this nice green landing area – the trees, the water, the deep rough that all the other players see.

You might be saying to yourself at this point, "John, that total visualization of *target only* sounds pretty good, but don't you need to be aware of the trouble, which side is not too bad to be on if you miss and which side is *jail*? That way you can favour the better side and lower your chance of getting in big trouble." Well, my answer is that on the surface, this thinking seems pretty reasonable, but in actual practice it will hurt you. Why? Because now you are to some degree visualizing trouble rather than just your landing area. That, quite simply, leads to steering rather than taking a big free hit. I guarantee you that the very fact that I focus only on my target area actually keeps me out of trouble, because it allows me to make my best swing a much higher percentage of the time. I simply would not be able to hit it long and straight as often as I do if I were doing anything except visualizing my target area.

My visualization process is basically the same when I'm in the fairway playing to the green on a par four or par five hole, or on the tee on a par three. The only difference is that instead of focusing on a distant area and trying to hit the ball as hard as I can, I focus on the flag itself, because what I really want to do is hole the shot. It's rare for me not to go for the pin. Even though most of the flags at PGA Tour events are pretty well guarded and are more or less on the corners of most greens, I'm almost always focusing on the flag rather than on the safe side of the green.

I admit that I have the luxury of playing to the pin almost exclusively because I possess a couple of big advantages. First, I probably hit the ball higher than anyone currently playing the game, so my approach shots drop onto the green at a steep angle and stop almost dead. Second, I play with a balata-covered, wound golf ball. By comparison, I understand that most amateurs are playing with two-piece surlyn balls. The wound balata ball carries more backspin than the two-piece surlyn, which also makes it stop faster. So I may be able to stop a ball stiff to a really tight pin where, because you don't hit the ball as high and your ball doesn't spin as much, you can strike a perfect shot and find that the ball won't hold such a small piece of green.

What I'm trying to tell you about your visualization on shots to the green, then, is this: If the pin is reasonably accessible to you, given your normal ball flight with the club you have in hand, definitely put your focus on that pin and nothing else. If, however, the pin is tucked on the front left of the green behind a big bunker, you're a two-iron distance away, and you consistently fade the ball, you must change your strategy. Visualize very intently a shot that starts dead at the flag, then fades naturally so that it lands a little to the right of the hole and finishes close to the centre of the green, leaving you with a twenty- or twenty-five-foot putt. This is not a cop-out; it does not mean you are visualizing trouble, but rather the best shot you can play in this particular circumstance.

I think you'll find that on most of the holes you play, you will be able to realistically visualize a shot to the flag itself, and this process will work wonders for your approach shots. It's fun to hit an iron shot close to the hole. As your visualization improves, you'll find yourself doing this a lot more often.

As I'm looking over the target prior to starting the backswing, I jockey myself around a bit, but it is with no conscious thought about how to swing the club. You could make the analogy that I'm like a boxer who is looking for an opening, then, once he finds it, sets himself so that he can deliver that knockout punch. I'm sort of moving around, too, staying relaxed but getting myself set to deliver a great golf swing to the ball. As

My pre-swing routine includes three *waggles of the club.*

I'm doing this and visualizing my target, I am alternately taking a look at the target and then waggling the club up and down. My own system, which by now I do on instinct, is to take four looks at my target, with three nice loose waggles of the club, one waggle between each look.

After the last look, I'm ready to start the club back. My trigger for starting the club back is to firm up my grip on the club very slightly. Remember, this doesn't ever mean tight. During my waggling my grip is very light; then, after my last look at the target, I firm it up ever so slightly and move into the backswing motion smoothly, with no hesitation whatsoever. From the moment I firm up the grip, I only have one thought, which has become pretty well publicized as my so-called mantra of the golf swing. That simple thought is, "*Grip it and rip it!*"

I'm not telling you that you should copy exactly the number of looks and waggles I take as I visualize the shot, but I do hope you'll work on developing a consistent pattern of nice easy motion prior to the swing, and make it become second nature to you. It will work wonders for the smoothness of your swing, and improved results are bound to follow.

I want to conclude this important chapter by telling you about something I use as a mental pick-me-up that is tied very closely to the visualization process which I believe you must develop to hit your best shots. I call this mental gimmick the "Four Fs" and I think about them often when I'm between shots on the course. My Four Fs are *Fortitude, Faith, Focus* and *Foxiness.* They are traits that I feel are necessary to meet the challenges that tournament golf presents to me almost every day, and I think they are necessary to allow you to perform your best every time you tee it up, too. Let me explain them to you:

FORTITUDE: Golf is not physically tough like professional football or hockey. But it can wear you down mentally, whether you're playing for big money on the PGA Tour or trying to win a match in your flight of the club championship. I constantly remind myself on the course to have fortitude, to persist, stay positive, and weather the storm that's presented by an especially tough course or the fact that I may not be having a particularly good day. You can't let whatever problems you have had up to the present moment have any influence on the shots that you still have to play. You can't afford to say, "I'm three down after nine holes, I'm going to get beaten badly in this match," any more than I can afford to say, "I'm three over par after nine holes, there's no way I can come back and finish with a decent score." The secret is to stay with that pure visualization of a perfect result on every shot and keep making that good free swing. That takes fortitude. Persist when the going seems toughest and you'll be amazed at how often the law of averages turns in your favour and the good shots start to flow.

FAITH is a close relative of fortitude. Once you have developed your setup and swing fundamentals, stick with them and have faith in them. The principles I'm describing will work for any golfer within the limitations of his or her athletic ability. You must have faith in what you're doing, especially if you are in the process of relearning the fundamentals. Don't let a few bad swings, or even a few bad rounds, throw you off the track and start you down the bad road of searching for gimmicks. Have faith in your swing.

FOCUS means keeping your mind exclusively where it needs to be on the course, and that means on hitting your next shot perfectly You don't have to worry about that hole on the back nine that gives you trouble, or even the next hole, which is a par five that you're hoping to birdie. Neither should you be thinking of the right cross you'd like to throw at that aggravating opponent of yours who's deliberately rattling change while you putt. Or any of the other little aggravations, real or imagined, that come up in the course of every round. All that is petty stuff that losers get all worked up about and winners ignore. Just focus on your next shot and how you're going to set up perfectly – grip it and rip it.

You should focus on each shot so intently that when you walk off the eighteenth green, you don't even realize that the round is over. That will mean you've really been focused.

FOXINESS is a term you don't hear associated with golf too often, but I remind myself to play foxy golf all the time. What I mean by this is that you should play the way that you know works best for you, even if some expert or know-it-all playing partner wants to tell you why you have to do it his way.

A good example of foxiness is my attitude toward visualization, which includes seeing only the distant landing area even if there is trouble fairly close by. Let your opponent outsmart himself by worrying about the hazard, while you just focus in so keenly on your target that you end up hitting it. That's the best way to be "dumb like a fox" on the golf course.

Keep reminding yourself of the Four Fs between shots and even when you're off the course, and you'll find that gradually you'll become a tougher and better player.

Well, we've covered quite a bit of ground regarding your setup positions and your best mental preparation prior to making the swing. Are you ready to rip it? I am, so let's go the next chapter.

DALY'S DOGMA

Play the Ball

Ball position is one of the most misunderstood elements of the setup. The fact is, if you play the ball too far forward or too far back in your stance, it's virtually impossible to hit a tee shot solidly and accurately.

When you play the ball too far forward – say, off your left instep or toe – you will tend to turn your body to the left to put the club behind the ball at address, thereby forcing your shoulders into an open position. This faulty address causes you to swing the club on an exaggerated out-to-in path (rather than an inside-square-inside path), cut across the ball at impact, and then hit the ball off line.

When you play the ball too far back in your stance, the tendency is to turn your body to the right when setting up to the ball, which forces your shoulders into a closed position. This faulty setup causes you to swing the club on an exaggerated in-to-out path, with the result being a wayward shot.

Because a small error in ball position makes a big difference in your shots, practice hitting tee shots until you are confident you are consistently playing the ball virtually off your left heel.

Get Ready, Get Set

If your setup is correct – feet, knees, hips, shoulders all lined up parallel to the target line – your tee shots will fly reasonably straight, even if you make a mediocre swing.

Correct alignment starts with a consistent pre-swing routine – a series of actions a golfer goes through to ready himself to swing and hit a shot. Too many club-level players hit poor shots because they set up haphazardly, sometimes even failing to focus on the target. Try not to do this. Remember:

1.Form a vivid picture of your actual target that is an area of fairway 240 yards in front of the tee.

2. Check that the clubface is dead square to your target and lined up with the back of your left hand.

3. Jockey your body into the classic parallel position without disturbing the alignment of the clubface.

Keep Your Distance

Many golfers realize that standing too far from the ball with both arms outstretched causes an overly flat swing plane and that standing too close to the ball causes an overly upright swing. Yet, ironically, they don't know what is the correct distance to stand in relation to the ball. If you are confused about this fundamental of the setup, here's a valuable tip: If your hands are outside your forehead at address, you are standing too far from the ball. If your hands are well inside the tip of your chin, you are standing too close to the ball.

Adapting to the Conditions

Golf is a game that demands that you sometimes change your setup and swing. Depending on whether you're hitting a drive or a punch wedge shot, for example, you will have to widen or narrow your stance or change your ball position.

The conditions of the day of your round matter, too. When the grass is wet from rain, you'll need to widen your stance slightly to promote a more compact swing and play the ball back to ensure clean clubface-to-ball contact.

How to Trim the "Fat"

If you're a golfer who has been plagued by the "fats" – contacting the grass well behind the ball and hitting the shot heavy – on short iron shots, try these tips:

1. Take a practice swing and see where the club contacts the grass. If it is well behind the spot where you have been

previously playing the ball, move the ball back in your stance.

2. Focus your eyes on the top of the ball instead of the back of it. This minor adjustment will automatically encourage you to shift a little more of your weight to your left side at address. In turn, this setup will encourage you to make a more upright backswing and clean sharp hit at impact.

Perfect Posture
Correct posture – standing comfortably erect with a slight bend in the knees and waist – is a vital element in employing a good golf swing. Yet many amateurs stoop over or stand too straight at address. To promote good posture, imagine that you are sitting on the edge of a barstool.

The Big Hit
My buzz phrase "grip it and rip it" will encourage you to hit the ball hard, but it will not hurt to have a couple of other power keys to draw on.

Imagine that a tee is suspended in the air horizontally, with its tip touching the back centre portion of the ball. Your mission, should you accept it, is to drive that tee through the ball at impact.

A second mental key to promote power is to imagine there is a cap taped to the back of the ball. Your goal is to hit the ball so solidly that the cap explodes at impact.

How to Overcome First-tee Nerves
A relaxed body and a confident mind are two very important keys to hitting the ball far down the fairway and dead at your target. The trouble is that most golfers become so overwhelmed by the crowd of friends or fellow members that congregate by the first tee that they become tense, think negatively, and hit a bad shot as a result.

To help you overcome first-tee jitters, see yourself making a smooth swing and hitting a perfect shot before you trigger the swing. Show yourself you can do it in your mind's eye. Then you won't care how many eyes are on you.

A Better Angle

The high clubhead speed that I normally generate is a result of a big turn of my upper body and a brisk release action of my hands and arms in the hitting area. However, if I really want to belt one, I make a tiny adjustment in my stance that makes a whole lot of difference in the distance the ball flies in the air.

I simply point my left foot out forty-five degrees instead of twenty-five degrees, from a position perpendicular to the target line.

Angling out my foot a little more automatically opens my left hip a little more, which means my hip clearing action on the downswing will be even faster, thereby allowing me to swing the club more freely into the ball at a much faster speed.

Line Up Your Hands Correctly

Golfers who lift the club abruptly at the start of the backswing are usually very bad long iron players. The reason is, a steep backswing makes for a sharp hit at impact, which is fine for playing the high-lofted irons in your bag, but not for hitting the less-lofted clubs that require a sweeping action.

If your long irons are landing well short of the green and well right of it, you are probably setting up with your hands a few inches in front of the ball. Try keeping your hands in line with the ball or a tad ahead of it.

Go for Broke

If you're one of those golfers who gets overly tense when the match gets close down the stretch, forget trying to hit an iron smoothly. If you face a six-iron shot, for example, take a seven-iron instead and hit it hard. You'll find that concentrating on making a killer swing will take your mind off the match, allowing you to hit a great shot close to the hole.

The Secret of Staying Calm

The typical amateur golfer often freezes over the ball, probably because he tries to recall some swing tip he read about in a golf magazine. When he finally comes out of his trance, he jerks the club away, loses his balance on the downswing, then hits a bad shot. Be like me: Don't ponder over a shot.

To help you make a smooth transition into the backswing, use a forward press, such as setting your hands level with the ball at address, then pressing them forward slightly and starting the backswing from there.

2
HOW TO BUILD A KILLER BACKSWING

I know that in the past, all of the young "long hitters" who have made a splash on the PGA Tour have been coached by some crafty veterans into gradually believing that in order to be really good players, they would have to cut down their natural swings so that they would increase their accuracy. I'm too foxy to listen to that advice; nobody is going to coach me out of an advantage that many of the players out here on the Tour would kill for!

Believe me, I'm not trying to boast; I'm just stating the facts. Make no mistake, the ability to out-hit your opponents, at any level of play, gives you an edge.

On the Tour level, what it means is that even during weeks in which my game is not that sharp, I may still come away with a good finish because under normal conditions, I can reach any par five on the Tour in two. So I pick up a few of what I consider bonus birdies, or maybe an eagle, during the course of a tournament that some other Tour players can't expect. On the weeks in which my timing is good and I've got my putter going, I am a definite threat to win the tournament.

On the club level, the advantage of hitting it further than you thought possible is just tremendous. Let's consider it in terms of sheer numbers first. Say you are a middle-handicap player and that you make pretty good contact, you can hit the driver about 220 yards. The other players hit it about the same length.

Now let's put you on a medium-length par four, say 400 yards. Suppose you hit a pretty good one off the tee – 220 down the middle. This leaves you with 180 yards to the pin – no easy position for someone with your length. You've got a pretty tough long iron shot or maybe a five-wood left to get home.

You've also got to remember something else if you're a middle-handicap player. You're not going to be in the fairway as often as you'd like. Let's take another example in which you again make pretty decent contact, sending the ball a good 220 yards, but you hook or pull the shot a little, so the ball ends up in the rough. Not only do you have to play a long shot from the rough, but you must play a slightly longer shot because you have hit the ball off-line. Remember that the 400-yard distance is measured as a straight line along the centre of the fairway to the green. Depending on how far left you've hit this one, you'll probably have somewhere between 190 and 200 yards to get home instead of 180. For you that's probably a perfect four-wood, but unless you catch a good lie you won't reach the green.

So you see, lack of distance is costing you the chance of getting home in regulation on many of the holes you play.

THE PHYSICAL (AND MENTAL) ADVANTAGES OF DISTANCE GAINS

Let's take a minute to think about what a realistic gain in distance can do for your golf game. When I say *realistic*, I mean a reasonable percentage of increase in distance with all clubs, obtained over a reasonable time with a reasonable amount of work. You can't get much longer overnight. But as long as you're in good health and willing to work at it, I know you can learn to be a longer hitter with a month or two of good effort.

Suppose you were able to add just 20 yards to your drives. That would be fun, wouldn't it? This increase, which is about 9.1 percent if you're a middle-handicap player, would put you out there about 240 yards. If you've hit the ball straight down the middle, you now have just 160 yards left to the flat.

Let's not forget, if you have now become over 9 percent longer with your driver, you'll also be more than 9 percent longer with your approach clubs. At your old length, you would have been between a four- and five-iron distance from the pin. But since you are 9 percent longer across the board, you're about 15 yards longer from this distance. So you're right in six-iron range to the flag. You're now playing this 400-yard hold with driver and six-iron instead of driver and long iron or lofted wood at your old distance.

I think the physical advantage of increased distance becomes even greater on those occasions when your ball lands in the rough. Your 240-yard drive into the rough leaves you 20 yards closer to the hole, of course. Now you've got 170 to 180 yards left (as opposed to 190 or 200 in the previous example). Instead of needing a perfect four-wood to get home (which would only be possible if the lie were good), you now will be playing either a four- or five-iron to the green. That's a big edge in itself. Remember, too, that your increased clubhead speed will make a big difference in your ability to get the clubhead through the ball, even if your lie is mediocre.

Finally, let's look at the mental advantage of hitting the ball longer. Say you've been playing with the same group for the last five or ten years, and you all hit the ball about the same distance. If over a couple of months' time you were to gain the distance advantage I just described, your foursome match would be a completely new ball game. If you got this much longer, believe me, you'd know you were going to beat them every time out. I know it sounds cocky to say this, but when you get a lot longer, you feel a lot better about yourself and you play the game with a lot more confidence. It will show in your demeanour, and the way you look at the golf course and want to attack it rather than play defensively. It may even intimidate your opponents.

Add this huge mental edge to the substantial physical advantage that I've just outlined, and the ball game's over with your golf group. Of course, you can still play with them, and of course they'll start demanding that you give them strokes to keep the game even. But you can live with that, can't you?

A SECRET TO BUILDING A LONG POWER SWING

Before we get into building a power backswing, I want to tell you a story that I think has much to do with the power game I have today. And it relates to you and how you can build more power into your backswing no matter how old you are, how long you've played, or how short you presently hit the ball.

I started whacking a plastic golf ball around in my backyard with a toy club not too long after I learned how to walk. When I was six, my father gave me my first set of clubs. Actually, it was an odd set that had been lying around in the garage, and it was a men's set. My dad didn't have enough money to buy me a perfectly fitted junior set, and besides, he thought about clubs like you do about wearing your big brother's old clothes – he'll grow into them.

So anyway, there I was at age six, trying to swing a man-sized driver. Not only was the club far too long for me, but it was far too heavy for me, too. It would be about the same as you, an adult, trying to swing a driver that is sixty inches long instead of forty-three inches, and that weighs something like thirty ounces instead of thirteen. And the iron clubs were heavier even though they were shorter, so for me they were just as bad.

The result was, these clubs were so long and heavy that they swung me. As the clubshaft neared the parallel position that most experts would say marks the completion of the backswing, the length of the shaft and weight of the clubhead carried my wrists, hands, arms, and shoulders around so much further that I must have looked like a real lemon! It was ridiculous, because at the top of my six-year-old's swing, sometimes the clubhead would even hit the ground next to my left foot.

Of course, I didn't hit many good shots like this, and probably a lot of golf teachers would have laughed at what they saw. But I believe that a very important thing was being ingrained in me at an early age, even though I had no idea it was happening at the time: My body was being trained to understand what a huge backswing turn felt like. Beyond the obvious loosening effect this clubhead weight had on my hands and wrists, those long, heavy clubs were making the muscles of my upper back, my torso, and even my hips stretch to the maximum.

Just like many other things in life, what is ingrained during the early years usually becomes a habit that stays with you through your adult life. I became used to the feeling of that heavy clubhead cocking my wrists and pulling my entire upper body way around. Swinging a club was pretty tiring back then, but I didn't know it wasn't supposed to be so tiring. I was just having a lot of fun.

Meanwhile, the great thing that was happening in those early years was that my spine was getting exceptionally flexible. Today, I may not look like a great athlete to you and I've been known to eat a few too many cheeseburgers, but I still have the great flexibility that allows me to make a super-strong backswing turn. And that is the key toward developing the newfound power that will make this game so much fun for you to play.

SWING A LONG, HEAVY CLUB

You can buy a weight-training golf club or, alternatively, make one on your own. Many professional shops and retail outlets sell weighted clubs that are usually the same length as, or maybe a couple of inches longer than, a standard men's driver. The clubhead, the shaft, or both are heavily weighted with sand or lead so that the club actually weighs about five times what a normal driver would – four to five pounds instead of thirteen to fourteen ounces.

To make your own weighted club, all you need is an old driver that you won't be using. First, remove the grip (if you haven't worked on clubs and are not sure of yourself, you can always have this done at a local repair shop). Pour a substantial amount of sand or lead pellets down the shaft, then weigh the club. If you are a man who is in reasonably good health and has average muscle tone, a club in the four- to five-pound range should be about right. For seniors and women, it's probably wise to scale back to about a three-pound club.

I recommend that for maximum benefit, you make the club a couple of inches longer than standard by adding a plug to the end of the shaft. A little extra length will add to the pulling effect at the top of the backswing, which is what you want. Finally, put a new grip over the end of the shaft.

Start swinging your training club a little every day in your backyard or indoor workout area. The key thing to remember is that you must swing the club very slowly and fully. Don't worry too much about your mechanics, but rather, concentrate on a very slow, fluid movement. Remember that you're swinging a super-heavy club. Trying to swing it at anything like normal speed could lead to injury.

As you slowly move the club into the backswing, you'll feel the weight of the clubhead and clubshaft working on your forearms. Later, after your arms have passed waist height and the clubshaft has passed perpendicular, you'll actually feel it begin to pull on your hips, your back, and your shoulders, so that they'll want to keep turning even further. Whatever the length your backswing is currently, the weight of your training club will encourage you to go beyond it. Don't try to decide in advance how much further you want to swing back than normal. Just let the training club do its work. Then, very slowly and smoothly, start the clubshaft back down, around and through the impact zone. Again, as you work your way into the follow-through, you will feel tension on your forearms, followed by a pull on your shoulders and torso into a very full finish position.

Start slowly with your weighted club training. Just make about a dozen slow swings a day the first week or so. Then add a few more slow swings per day the second week, and a few more the next, until you're making about twenty swings a day. You'll find that over time, that weight at the top of the backswing will pull you around a little further and a little further still. If you continue this exercise over, say, two months, you just won't believe how much turn you'll have added to your backswing.

This is a particularly good way to train for those of you who live in the northern parts of the country. Start working with the weighted club at the end of one season and I'll guarantee you a bigger backswing turn and a lot more power the following spring.

THE MECHANICS OF A POWERFUL BACKSWING

The golf swing is simply one big, continuous turning motion. I just keep turning back away from the ball as far as I can go, so that my body actually springs into a downswing turn, which I also make as far as I can go. I use this image of a continuous turn on all my full shots, from the driver down to a full sand wedge. I believe you should do the same.

Let's take a look at some of the particulars that should occur as you execute the backswing. As we discussed in Chapter One, I finish my preshot preparation by taking four looks at my target, interspersing three waggles of the clubhead between them. Then I very slightly increase the pressure in my grip as a signal to draw the club back.

Strive to push the club away from the ball very slowly and low to the ground, straight back from the ball for the first foot or so. You should have the sensation that if anything, the left hand is controlling this initial movement of the clubhead. The reason I suggest this is that any quick pickup of the clubhead, which is usually initiated with the right hand, works against building the wide arc you'll need if you're going to hit the ball powerfully.

You can't take the clubhead away from the ball too slowly. I know that Jack Nicklaus has stated in the past that whenever he was looking to hit an extra-big drive, he would make certain to start the clubhead back even more slowly than usual. And Jack has always had one of the slowest takeaways in the game to begin with. That should tell you something. You'll never hit the ball with your backswing. Just keep the takeaway as slow as possible with the left hand pushing straight back, to give you a start toward the widest possible swing arc.

As you begin the takeaway, you should not make any independent manipulation of the clubhead with your hands. The clubface must start straight back from the ball. A lot of golfers, even a few on the pro tours, are under the impression that they must do something to get the clubhead inside the target line at some point. You don't have to concern yourself with this at all. As you continue to push the clubhead away from the ball, it will very gradually and naturally begin to turn to the inside of the target line. The very simple reason it will do this is that you are standing to one side of the ball. Although we will talk in great detail later about "flat" and "upright" swing planes, for now all you need to understand is that it's impossible to keep the clubhead on the target line throughout the swing. To some degree, the clubhead must move inside the target line as the backswing progresses, and it will do so without any independent hand action from you.

TURN, DON'T SWAY

As my takeaway continues, I focus on turning my right side away from the ball as fully as possible. Notice that I said *turning* rather than *moving* my right side. A powerful, repeating golf swing should always be based on turning as fully as possible around a fixed centre, as opposed to shifting the body weight in a side-to-side lateral motion. This fixed centre point is your spine, which is the central axis of your golf swing. All of the powerful winding movement we have talked about must move in a circular way around your spine, rather than allowing your upper body to move laterally on the backswing.

The reason I've urged you to swing a weighted club is that in order to make the excellent turn around a fixed axis, you'll need as much flexibility as you can muster. The error that a large majority of amateurs make on the backswing is that they sway to the right. When the body weight moves to the outside of the right foot, you may feel as though you're developing some power to put into the shot on the downswing, but you'll never build as much power with a sway as you will with a good honest turn. Why? When you sway you can't make a good turn around your spine. Furthermore, if your body sways laterally off the ball on the backswing, it has to move laterally toward the target (sway) on the downswing by exactly the same amount in order to make perfect contact. So, obviously, a sway breeds lots of inconsistency as well as your loss of power.

As you hands continue to move beyond your right knee and approach hip height, you'll begin to feel your body weight, which was fifty-fifty between the feet at address, begin to shift onto your right foot. The key to continuing to make a turn rather than a sway is to keep your weight on the inside of your right foot as the backswing progresses. It's easy to let the right knee buckle out and the weight move to the outside of the right foot, particularly early on in the swing. However, as you can see in the photographs overleaf, at the midpoint of my backswing, my right leg is still straight, rather than bowed out to the right. About 75 percent of my weight is on my right foot at this point; however, it is on the inside of my foot and will continue to stay there throughout the backswing.

The reason I'm going into so much detail about not letting the weight move to the outside of the right foot is that it's a common problem for power golfers. It may also be for you as you strive to increase your distance. You see, with the low, slow, wide swing arc that you're striving for, there will be more of a tendency for your weight to be pulled onto the outside of your right foot. If you just picked up the club quickly with your arms and hands in a narrow arc, you probably wouldn't have to worry about any sway. However, this type of backswing hinders your turning action and this plays havoc with your distance potential. So it's better to work toward building a wide backswing arc while being aware of keeping your weight shift under control.

Actually, I can speak from extensive experience about swaying off the ball because I used to do it quite a bit myself. I sure didn't want to sway, but I fell into the habit as I was trying to build as big a backswing arc as possible. And I'm here to tell you, when your weight gets too far to the outside of your right

Turning into a braced right leg and loading your weight on the inside *of your right foot is a critical link to generating power.*

foot on the backswing, where the shot is going to finish becomes a real lottery. You may return to the ball just right so you hit it straight; you may hang back on your right side on the downswing, with the usual result being a big hook; or you might end up with the same result I found most often, a pronounced sway back to the left on the downswing, causing the body to get ahead of the ball at impact. The result of this move is a shot that's hit solidly but flies to the right of the target.

If you can keep your weight on the inside of your right foot, you'll build a much stronger coil and your shots will fly straight and far. You'll find, as I did, that you'll need to train your right foot to keep the weight to the inside. Once I became convinced that I had to overcome this backswing flaw, I spent many hours on the practice tee, hitting the longer clubs while making sure that at no point in the backswing did my weight get beyond the centre of my right foot – even with a big driver swing. This is hard work. After several hundred balls, the inside of my right foot, ankle, and lower calf would be the most tired part of my whole body. I was building up the strength in this area that I needed to hold my weight there throughout the backswing. The effort was well worth it, though, because my lower right leg and foot muscles are now trained so that I rarely, if ever, sway off the ball.

Chances are that as you build a powerful turn into your backswing, you'll also need to work on keeping that weight on the inside of your right foot. I don't expect you to hit as many balls as I do. But if you think you might be swaying or your friends observe that you are, you'll just have to force yourself to let that weight shift only to the inside of your right foot, while still making a very low, slow takeaway with your left arm in control of the club. If, after your practice sessions, you feel tired on the inside of the right foot and lower leg, that's good. It means you're building the strength that will help you make a big turn, yet stay in control of your swing.

TAKING IT TO THE TOP: CONTINUE THE COIL

It may sound as if I'm breaking down the backswing into a number of parts and that there are a multitude of things for you to think about in executing it. Ultimately, this won't be the case. You'll be able to think of the backswing as I do – that is, that it's just one big turn. But I want you to understand the areas in which problems can arise so that you can correct them if they creep into your game. Once you practice the right moves enough after correcting any backswing flaws you might have now, the repetitions will again build the backswing into a single continuous unit.

Now you're halfway through the backswing, and you've built the foundation of a wide swing arc while keeping your weight shift under control. From this point, I think in terms of turning my back as far as I possibly can, so that it faces the target at the top of the swing. Actually, in my case, the upper part of my back turns a little way beyond pointing at the target. That is, my shoulder turn goes beyond 90 degrees, to about 110 degrees with the driver.

There is no limit to how far you should turn on the backswing. If you can turn your shoulders 140 degrees, then turn them 140 degrees. You would probably be able to drive some par fours if you could do that. And, I must admit, you'd also be some kind of freak of nature. But my point is, on any full shot, never limit yourself as far as your backswing turn is concerned. The degree of shoulder turn is the number one thing that's lacking in the swings of most amateurs.

I'll bet there are a lot of you who, for whatever reason, don't turn your shoulders more than fifty degrees in the backswing. It's truly a technical must that you increase your shoulder turn if you are going to increase the power in your swing. That's why I want you to swing a weighted club and do the exercises I recommend in the Daly's Dogma at the end of this chapter. If you currently turn only fifty degrees and find the best you can do is increase it to seventy degrees, you'll see a big distance improvement. If your shoulders currently turn just seventy degrees and you can get that up to eighty, you, too, will hit the ball much longer. And if you've got a fairly decent shoulder turn right now, say eighty degrees, and your workouts allow you to increase that turn to ninety degrees, you'll be amazed at your power increase.

In addition to your efforts to improve your backswing physically, just knowing that you should turn as far as possible will help you to make an increase. The mind will help the body do what it is focusing on. So keep on turning that spine just as far as you can.

As you continue turning your shoulders up into their fullest coil, remember to keep turning your hips as far as possible, in the same clockwise manner. There are some pros who teach a theory of resistance by the hips – that is, keeping the hips from turning while at the same time making the big shoulder turn. The idea here is that you will build up a tremendous amount of torque between your upper body and your lower body, right at the waist, which you will then automatically unleash into a powerful downswing action.

I don't agree with this resisting-the-hips reasoning. Instead, I think you should turn them along with your shoulders as far as possible. First, I think that trying to coil one part of your body fully while resisting with another is too complicated for the average player (or even myself) to coordinate successfully. Second, I believe that the full-body turn ultimately unleashes a more powerful downswing release than the resisting-hips backswing does, for reasons we'll talk about in the next chapter.

So turn the hips as fully as possible. Because of the makeup of the human body you'll never be able to turn your hips as far as your shoulders. However, assuming you have no physical problems and that you do have reasonable flexibility, I'd like to see your hips turn two-thirds as far as your shoulders turn on the backswing. For example, if you are able to turn your shoulders a full ninety degrees, then your hip turn ideally would be sixty degrees.

As you're making this full-body coil, your lower body will be in motion, too. Really, the motion in your legs is more of less a reaction to a full shoulder and hip turn.

To promote power there should be two noticeable movements by the left leg during the backswing. (The right leg, meanwhile, remains as stable as possible, holding the weight on the inside of the leg.) First, as the backswing reaches and goes beyond the midway point, your left knee should begin to be pulled inward, to the right, so that by the time you reach the top of the backswing, it points behind the ball (to the right of it as you are looking down).

This inward pulling of the left knee is simply a reaction to the upper body coil. You should not consciously rotate your left knee so that it points behind the ball. If you do notice that your left knee is not automatically being pulled so that it points behind the ball, it's a signal that your upper body is not turning nearly far enough. Don't attempt to make a fake inward movement with the left knee because that movement, made on its own, doesn't do you any good. Instead, work on increasing that full-body turn.

The second movement is the lifting of the left heel that takes place as you approach and reach the top of your backswing. Again, this is a natural reaction to the increased turn you're now making. Because your hips are turning quite a way along with your shoulders, it will become impossible to keep your left heel planted as it was during the address and takeaway. It has to be pulled up by the upper body and hip turn.

Now, I know that a lot of teachers along the way have said that in order to retain maximum balance and body stability throughout the swing, you should keep the left heel planted from start to finish. I strongly disagree with this theory, particularly when you're swinging the longer clubs. If you determine that you're going to keep your left heel on the ground, you should have a pretty reliable base for your swing. But you will also be

If you seek a long swing and a long ball, turn your hips and shoulders to the maximum.

If your upper body turns correctly on the backswing, your left knee will be pulled inward automatically.

severely limiting the amount of backswing turn you can make. And, as I said earlier, you need to make as big a turn as your physique allows. Unless you happen to be Superman, you can't afford to limit the power you generate in this game.

You may have heard of other instructors who say it's okay if the left heel rises on the backswing, as long as it's not "too much." I believe that as long as you keep that resistance on the inside of your right foot so that you don't sway off the ball, it doesn't matter how far the left heel rises. If your turn is so big that it pulls your left heel an inch and a half off the ground, as long as you are retaining your balance, I think that's great. In his absolute prime while swinging the driver, Jack Nicklaus lifted his heel probably about three inches. I'll bet Jack wishes it came up that high now. It doesn't, because in his fifties, Nicklaus is not able to duplicate the huge turn he made in his early twenties.

My own left heel probably doesn't rise quite as much as Jack's did – with the driver I'd say it is pulled up about two inches. The distance the heel is pulled up will be a little more or a little less from one individual to the next, depending on how flexible each person is. The more flexible you are, the less the heel will rise, and vice versa.

Keep in mind, though, as with the movement of the left knee, the raising of the left heel must be in reaction to the upper body turn. It must never be done independently. I see a lot of weaker-hitting amateurs, most of whom appear to be beginners, who make almost no backswing turn at all but who pick up their left heel as they take the club back. These golfers must have read somewhere that the left heel should rise on the backswing, but they sure don't look like they're making a golf swing to me; instead, it looks like some kind of ballet move.

The good power golf swing is not some kind of silly dance routine. Focus on building the maximum shoulder and hip turn your physique will allow. Let the left knee respond by pointing behind the ball, and let the left heel rise the amount it needs to in response to your turn, while keeping good balance. If you can do these things you will have improved your backswing tremendously.

Let your strong body coil force your left heel to lift off the ground.

THE "WINGING" RIGHT ELBOW

We have pretty well covered the movement of your body during the backswing, so now I'd like to get into what your arms and hands should be accomplishing as you stretch the club up to the top and beyond parallel.

The majority of teachers preach that as the club approaches the top of the backswing, your arms should remain relatively tight to your body. They suggest that your hands and arms should remain in a rather low position, with your firm left arm remaining at or below the angle at which your shoulders have turned away from the ball. When your left arm is in this position, they note, your right arm will be very much tucked in to your right side, with the right elbow pointing more or less down. A checkpoint that these theorists like to use is that if you are in what is often termed a "connected" position, you would be able to place a handkerchief underneath your right armpit and then make a complete backswing without the handkerchief dropping out.

If you look at the side-view photograph (overleaf) of my backswing, you may note that I've swung my arms on a plane that would be considered upright. That is, my arms have swung above the angle on which my shoulders have turned, so that at the very top of the swing my hands are more above my head than they are behind me.

In a minute, I'll tell you why I try to reach for this upright position and why I think it will benefit you. For now, let me tell you how to reach it.

As I'm making that full turn with my body, I simply tell myself to reach for the sky with my hands. This reaching sensation is quite simple to achieve if you take the club away as I recommended, straight back from the ball, low to the ground, and with your left hand and arm controlling the action. To some degree your body build will determine how high or upright you can swing your hands – the tall player who stands closer to the ball at address can naturally make a more upright backswing than the shorter player. However, I'm under six feet tall and I manage to make a very upright arm swing, so it definitely can be done. Just turn your body as fully as you can as you push your hands and arms upward toward the sky.

I'd like to point out one other thing that occurs when you execute this upright arm swing. My right elbow is more up and away from my body than it is in that tucked-in position that many teachers advocate. Instead of pointing downwards, the elbow points pretty much behind me. And no, I definitely can't hold a handkerchief under my arm at the top of the backswing. But let's leave the major tricks to others and do what we can to help you hit good golf shots.

Above: Swinging your arms high will allow you to whip the club down into a ball at high speed and make a more direct hit at impact.
Right: To promote a strong, upright swing, push your hands toward the sky at the top of the backswing.

This "flying" or "winging" right elbow is the source of a lot of controversy in the golf swing. It's been stated many times that a winging elbow means that the swing is not on plane, that it's too upright. Well, I just don't accept the theory that there is one perfect plane on which everybody should swing the club. Ben Hogan swung the club on a plane that even the perfect-plane theorists would have said was too low or too flat. However, while I don't like a flat plane, either, I understand Hogan was a pretty good player.

Of course, early in his career my role model, Jack Nicklaus, had a really upright swing. His right elbow winged out more than mine does today. I understand that Jack was really taken to task for this apparent flaw. However, Jack "only" managed to win eight major championships by the time he was just twenty-six, so that did silence a lot of people. And it went to prove that his upright swing worked. Here are two big reasons why I think it will work for you:

1. The more upright arm swing will keep the club moving more along the target line than will the flatter swing. The flatter the swing, the more important it will become that the clubhead contacts the ball at the precise moment at which it is travelling parallel to the target line. This flatter swing makes it all the more important that your ball position at address be perfect – if it's too far back, you'll push the shot, and if it's too far forward, you'll pull it. When you deliver the clubhead from a more upright angle, it won't matter as much whether you ball position is perfect, because the clubhead is not deviating as much from a path that's more along the target line.

2. I think it's a very much overlooked fact that the upright arm swing will make you a much more effective player out of the rough. Any swing plane can be effective when you're hitting the ball from a good lie in the fairway. But the upright swing gives you a big edge when you miss the fairways. The reason is, when your club approaches the ball from this more upright angle, there's less chance that long grass can wrap around the hosel of the club and slow its momentum, muffling the shot. Also, with the upright swing, less grass intervenes between the clubface and the ball at impact so that you can impact more backspin and control to your shots.

It's important to be realistic about what type of swing you need in order to work your ball around the golf course most effectively. Most amateurs don't realize that they're hitting a lot more shots from the rough than they are from the fairway. Look at it this way. Even the most accurate drivers on the PGA Tour hit only 70 to 75 percent of the fairways. The less accurate drivers on the Tour hit maybe 55 to 60 percent of the fairways. So be realistic. How many fairways can you expect to hit per round?

Sure, you'd like to hit as high a percentage as you can, and I think after you begin to apply the principles provided here, you will hit more fairways because you'll be hitting the ball more squarely. But it pays to realize that you're going to be in the rough sometimes. Therefore, the upright arm swing will really help you hit more greens from the rough. It will also at least ensure that you'll get the ball out of deep grass and advance it further than you possibly could have with a flatter swing.

Looking at it over the course of a season, you just won't believe how many strokes this added capability will save you when playing from the deep stuff.

So strive to get your hands high at the top of your swing and don't pay any mind to whether you're winging that right elbow.

Letting the right elbow fly on the backswing is a must for a solid, upright action.

CROSSING THE LINE: WHY IT'S OK

Suppose you've done everything I've suggested so far and have made a much-improved, more wound-up, fuller backswing. You may be thinking that you're really ready to "rip it," and in reality you are. However, here again you may be in for some criticism from any standard swing theorists you play with, who may now point out to you that you're "crossing the line" at the top of your backswing.

First, let me explain what the term *crossing the line* means. Second, I'll tell you why it often occurs (naturally) in the full-turn golf swing. And third, I want to state my case as to why it's all right for you to cross the line.

At the top of your backswing the clubshaft is on the line if it's pointing exactly parallel to the target line. Generally this is considered to be the most desirable position to be in, under the premise that there's no need to manipulate the club on the downswing to produce a square hit.

If your club were to point to the left of the target at the top of the backswing, you'd be in what is termed a "laid-off" position. Not too many teachers would favour this position because when your clubshaft is pointing to the left of target, it means that your hands are somewhat closer to the target line than you'd like them to be, and the clubhead is farther away from it (more to the left). From this position, it's easy for your right shoulder and your hands to come over the ball from the outside in. This usually results in a slice, although for the better golfer it's often a pull or pull-hook. However, the results are never carved in stone. Ben Hogan played from a slightly laid-off top-of-backswing position and hit the ball awfully well.

Now, if your clubshaft crosses or points to the right of the target line at the top, you are crossing the line. It's been argued that the path of the club on the downswing will tend to mirror the line the clubshaft is pointing toward at the top, so if anything, you are likely to swing through the ball from the inside out. This starts the ball to the right of the target line and usually puts a right-to-left spin on the ball so that a draw or a hook will then result.

If you were to look at the top-of-swing positions of today's top pros from behind the target line, you would notice that the majority of them, including myself, cross the line. And this isn't too surprising because as you probably know, most Tour players can draw the ball easily – partly because they get into this position at the top.

There are two reasons why I think it's okay that you cross the line at the top, beyond the simple fact that I and many other pros cross the line. First, I think that the longer the backswing you can make, the greater the likelihood that your

If you cross the line like I'm doing here, hitting a power draw shot will be easy.

clubshaft will naturally cross the target line. And second, I'm advocating that you develop the biggest possible turn and the longest backswing you can, crossing the line is just a natural result of accomplishing this. Second, the more upright an arm swing you make, the more likely you are to cross the line a bit at the top. That's because in an upright swing, the right elbow flies away from the body, and when it does, the hands turn to the right in relation to the target line. Since the hands are holding onto the club, this also automatically points the clubshaft more to the right in relation to the target line – in the classic cross-the-line position. Now that I've explained all this, I want to remind you to go back and stick to the backswing principles I've outlined earlier in this chapter. You don't have to worry whether you're crossing the line or not. The clubshaft will naturally take care of itself.

KEEP WRISTS LOOSE AT THE TOP

The last backswing point I'd like to talk about is the positioning of your wrists at the top. Actually, I'm not as much concerned with the positioning as I am that you keep them loose and relaxed, because this will naturally add power to your shots.

As I've said, very few people can match the length of my backswing. That's primarily true because of the tremendous body turn I make. It's also because I've been blessed with very supple wrist joints and I make the most of them by allowing my wrists to cock to the max at the very top of the swing.

When I say "cocking the wrists", I'm referring to an upward movement of the wrists, while holding your hands in front of you with the palms facing one another. Don't confuse cocking of the wrists with any side-to-side hinging that you can also do from this hands-in-front palms-together position.

When this cocking motion is allowed at the top of the backswing, the wrists are actually cocking downward because your hands are now above and behind you. Of course, as the wrists cock down, the clubshaft angles down quite a few degrees more than it would if the wrists remained stiff. An extra ten degrees of wrist cock would mean that the clubhead will travel a much longer distance as the backswing completes itself.

Naturally, some golfers can produce a greater degree of wrist cock than others. Again, my own wrists happen to be pretty flexible and so they cock downward quite a bit, adding greatly to the length of my backswing with the driver. Even if you can't cock your wrists this much, it will help to remind yourself to keep your grip pressure light on the club at all points of the swing, including at the top. Don't try to control the club's position at the top with additional pressure from your hands.

With a full turn of the shoulders and hips, a nice high arm swing, good balance with most of your weight staying to the inside of your right foot, and a nice light grip that lets the club hang freely at the top, you're in a great position to give the ball a bigger rip than even you might have though possible. With that in mind, let's see just what's needed on the downswing to complete a dynamic full-swing package.

This page and opposite: Cocking your wrists downward *at the top of your swing will programme added power into your drives.*

DALY'S DOGMA

Sway Prevention

Moving the body away from the target laterally on the backswing in such an exaggerated fashion that weight shifts to the outside of your right foot is a common fault of amateur golfers that leads to mishit shots.

If a friend has told you that you have this problem or you have seen yourself sway on video, practice hitting shots with a golf ball lodged under the right side of your instep. This will encourage you to keep your weight on the inside of your right foot during the backswing, which is exactly where it should be to ensure that you stay steady over the ball and coil into a braced right leg.

Forget the Parallel At-the-top Position

I'm not a historian of golf instruction; however, I strongly disagree with the teacher or professional who first advised a student to swing the club back to the parallel position (clubshaft parallel to the target line at the top of the backswing). It also annoys me that some modern-day teachers have called this the "classic" position.

Trying to arrive and stop in the parallel position at the top is so hard to do that it causes the player to lift the club on too steep an angle or to pause so long at the top that he finds it very difficult to make a smooth transition into the downswing.

Don't worry if you go beyond the parallel position. Just tell your teacher John Daly said it was all right.

Lift Off

Many golfers over fifty years of age lack the flexibility of younger players. Yet some seniors who don't accept this fact try to make a big swing, resulting in back injuries. Consequently, they must put their game on hold or, in some cases, quit.

You don't have to quit golf. Furthermore, you don't have to stop trying to make the big swing, provided you stop staying flat-footed during the motion. That's what's causing you to feel tight.

Let your left heel lift of the ground on the backswing as you turn your body, and see how much bigger your backswing becomes.

Let Your Left Arm Bend

One of the myths of golf instruction is that you must keep your left arm still during the backswing. No wonder so many golfers can't swing the club back far enough and look so robotic. All this advice does is cause the golfer to tense up, and when you're tight you can't generate sufficient clubhead speed to bring the club powerfully into the ball at impact.

Many of the greatest names of the past and some of today's living legends allow the left arm to bend. I know I do; it puts an added springiness in my hands and wrists and allows me to catapult the club into the ball on the downswing. So the next time you go out to practice or play, allow your left arm to bend as late as possible on the backswing.

The Proper Path

The most common takeaway faults are pulling the club back on an exaggerated inside path or pushing it back on a path well outside the target line.

The proper path for the club to swing along initially is straight back along the target line. To help you start the club on the proper path, imagine that you're dragging it through a foot-long trough of molasses that starts behind the ball and extends back along the target line.

Correct Your Reverse

If you "reverse pivot" – tilt your weight toward the target on the backswing, then rock it back away from the target on the downswing – you're probably moving your head toward your shoulder instead of keeping your head still and waiting for your left shoulder instead of keeping your head still and waiting for your left shoulder to rotate under your chin. Bear in mind that your head weighs about twenty pounds, so if you move it toward the target, it's no wonder your weight shifts improperly to the left side on the backswing.

To help you keep it steady and shift your weight correctly to your right side, focus your eyes on a spot directly behind the ball and stare intently at it until your left shoulder brushes your chin.

Turn Your Back on the Target
Coiling the upper body like a spring on the backswing is a critical link to power and a vital part of the swing's chain reaction. The more wound up you are, the faster your uncoiling action on the downswing. The faster your uncoiling action, the faster the speed of the clubhead. The faster the speed on the clubhead, the further the ball travels.

The weekend golfer has so many technical thoughts in his head that he gets confused on how to trigger the windup action. If you do, too, this tip should allow you to more easily coil your upper body like a pro: Turn your back to your target.

Get Physical, Get Flexible
Before your weekend round or rounds, here are a few simple exercises I strongly recommend you get in the habit of doing before you head out to the course. I do these exercises, as do Jack Nicklaus and other top professionals, for the simple reason that they enable you to stretch and losen your stiff muscles and therefore enhance your body coil.

– TOE TOUCHES. You can do these either from a standing position or by sitting on the floor with your legs stretched out in front of you. I usually do this exercise sitting on the floor, with my feet roughly a shoulder width apart.

Start by stretching both arms slowly toward your left big toe, and try to reach you left toe with the fingers of both hands. If you can't reach it, fine – just extend your fingers as far as you can and hold them there for a few seconds before relaxing back from that stretched position. Next, reach your fingers toward your right big toe as far as you can, holding that stretched position for about five seconds, then relax.

Repeat this stretch-and-hold exercise. You may notice that on the second go, you're able to reach about an inch further toward your toes than you did on the first shot, which means your spine is starting to limber up.

Repeat this exercise a third and final time. You might find your fingers reaching slightly further still this time around. Remember to hold the stretched position, rather than bouncing in an attempt to reach further, as holding the position will prevent you from straining a muscle.

– **THE "CRUNCH"**. Having just stretched the spine out, stretch your spine in by doing the following: From the position on the floor where you just finished stretching, draw your knees up and in, as close to your chest as possible. Then wrap your arms around your knees; and with your head down, "crunch" yourself in as tightly as possible, holding that position for a minimum of five seconds.

– **SIDE BENDS**. Lie down on the floor with your feet flat on the ground and your knees up. Place your arms at your side in a relaxed position with the palms down. Now slowly turn your knees to the left. Try to make your left knee reach the floor while keeping your back, shoulders, and hands flat on the floor.

You'll find that in trying to reach the floor with your knee, your right shoulder and your right hand will want to pull away from the flat positions. Keep your back and your right hand flat. Just work your legs (and with them, your hips and midsection) as far to the left as possible and hold that position for three seconds. Then swing your knees slowly in the opposite direction, trying to reach the floor with your right knee, while keeping your left upper back and your left hand flat on the floor. Hold this stretch for three seconds. Then repeat these side bends for a total of five minutes in each direction.

When you finish this brief set of exercises, I recommend that you take a hot shower. Let me tell you why.

A couple of years ago I read an article about Kevin Mitchell, the baseball batter on the Seattle Mariners team, who is annually at or near the top of the major league home run list. In this article, Mitchell said he had adopted the habit of taking a hot shower before each game. He believed that a steady ten-minute burst of warm water hitting his back and neck muscles really relaxed him, with the result that his baseball swing was noticeably looser and more flowing during the game that followed. And, as you will see throughout this book, I'm in favour of anything that promotes smooth rhythmic movements in the golf swing. So do what I do: Follow Mitchell's advice and you'll find it very helpful to the flow of your golf swing.

3

GO AHEAD AND RIP IT

We've almost reached the moment of truth, that vital instant when clubface meets ball and you either watch your shot soar high, straight, and long – or gape in dismay as the ball veers quickly off course and leaves you in trouble. Believe me, if you have ingrained the correct posture and alignment techniques and have put yourself in position with a great backswing turn, you are ninety percent along toward hitting an excellent power shot.

There's not much you have to think about in order for your downswing, impact position, and follow-through to be top-notch. The downswing happens so fast, there isn't time to do much thinking. More than anything, I believe it's important for all golfers to maintain an aggressive mind-set as they bring the club down and through the hitting zone.

As a worldwide golf traveller, I see many amateur golfers who, for one reason or another, just do not seem to be aggressive through the ball. Have you ever noticed players like these? They look like pros as they analyse the shot, set up to the ball, and make a beautiful, flowing backswing. Then, I don't know why this happens, but they seem to try to push or steer the clubhead through the impact zone, rather than use the good turn they've made and freewheel through the ball. The result is a definite loss of clubhead speed and poor point of impact, so they not only lose distance but hit the ball wildly, too. Short, wild tee shots are a disadvantage you just can't make up for.

You frequently hear about golfers who are plagued with so much fear on the putting greens that they develop the "yips." That is, they can't draw the putterblade back from the ball and

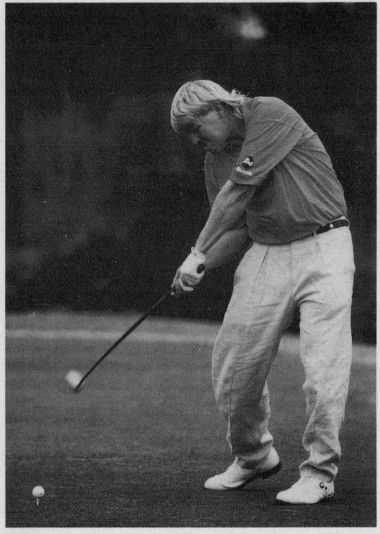

Above and opposite: The one thought that will help you come into impact more aggressively and hit through the ball powerfully, as I'm doing here, is "let it rip."

stroke smoothly through it so that the blade stays on the target line. It's pretty much agreed that the yips are caused by a lack of confidence that golfers develop over a long period of time, until they eventually believe that something bad is going to happen whenever the putter is drawn back. They get so nervous that they flinch instead of accelerating through the putt in the same way they should on a full shot.

I mention this because I believe that a good many golfers, whether they know it or not, have a case of the yips with the driver. Probably because of bad mechanics over the years, they've watched many tee shots sent either out of bounds, into water hazards, or into the trees. They realize that their driver swing is costing them quite a few shots per round and they are concerned enough that it really bugs them. After a while, they become so anxious that they make a short, tense backswing, then sort of stab at the ball on the downswing, just like the yipper does on the greens. The ball might be smothered, sliced, popped up, topped – anything but hit solid and straight.

I can't prove that even good golfers can yip their drives, but experience tells me it happens often. Otherwise, why do so many players hit great-looking drives on the practice tee, but suddenly start hitting the ball all over the golf course? They just aren't swinging through the ball with the nice, smooth, free-wheeling action they're capable of.

Before we get into the simple downswing moves to help you hit the ball long and straight, I'd like to urge you to change your attitude about driving, particularly if you're one of those closet yippers with the long stick. Stop being so nervous about where you don't want the ball to go, and within the boundaries of maintaining good balance, give the ball a good belt.

Driving the ball should be a lot of fun. It might help your confidence to think of the driver as an "area" club rather than a precision club. You don't have to stop the ball on the spot like you do with a wedge to a tight pin position. Instead, on most holes, you have a fairway that's about forty yards wide. Additionally, on the majority of holes, you have ten or more yards of open rough on either side of the fairway that, once you've built more power into your swing, really shouldn't be that much of a concern. So that's usually about sixty yards of space for you to hit your 1.68-inch ball into. You'll accomplish this goal if you trust your swing.

PLANT THE LEFT HEEL

You've put yourself in a strong, fully coiled position at the top. Your shoulders should be turned at least ninety degrees with a hip turn of about sixty degrees, you're holding that shifted weight on the inside of your right foot, and your wrists are nice and loose at the top so that the clubhead is handing nicely.

Now put the downswing into gear with one simple move – slam your left heel firmly back down into the ground.

This one simple move practically guarantees a good aggressive move into and then through the ball. The reason? You've built up a great deal of tension in that complete body coil at the top. By literally slamming that left heel back down, you have stretched the left side of your body so much that you are virtually forced to swing the club down. There's so much tension in your left side at this instant that you couldn't hold yourself in the proper sequence of motion must follow. Your left-heel slam pulls down your left leg and hip, your left hip pulls on your midsection, your midsection pulls on your shoulders, and your shoulders pull on your arms. Last, your arms will pull on your hands and your hands will begin to bring the clubhead downward from the top-of-the-swing position, with the clubhead approaching the ball from inside the target line.

Now, remember, you don't have to make your various body parts do all the things I just mentioned. If you have build enough lively tension into your backswing, then when you slam

As I illustrate here, replanting your left heel at the start of your downswing will automatically allow the club to achieve maximum speed in the hitting area.

down your left heel, the power you will generate literally can't be stopped. That the beauty of it – the downswing basically becomes a reaction rather than a planned delivery of the clubhead. And you know, I think it's actually good to make a "brain-dead" downswing, rather than one in which you're trying to think the club into the ball. Because once you slam that left heel down to commence the downswing, there's too little time left to do much thinking anyway.

KEEP CLEARING THE HIPS

There is another important movement I'd like you to be aware of that you should make certain you're accomplishing through the downswing. The move I am referring to is a very level, counterclockwise turning of your hips throughout the downswing. That is, your hips continue to move around in a circular fashion, to the left, on the downswing, just as they turned in a circular fashion to the right on your backswing. Of course, you may already be executing this move perfectly and if that's the case, fine. If not, however, a little change in your perception of your lower-body movement can enhance your release at impact.

It's a mistaken opinion that at impact you should look just like you did at address. As I'll explain in a moment, if your hips return to a square position at impact, it will cause you problems. At any rate, by impact my hips will have turned at least fifty degrees around or to the left of that square position they were occupying prior to the takeaway.

You're probably wondering why the hips should turn this far. There are three good reasons. First, a full, ongoing counterclockwise hip turn continues and indeed increases the release momentum you started by slamming down the left heel. The end result of the chain reaction of this body pull is that the clubhead will continue to accelerate through and beyond impact.

A second benefit is that continuing to lead the downswing with the movement of your lower body assures you that your hands and arms will remain the last link in the release chain. So, there will be no urge for you to make the mistake of trying to create power with your shoulders, arms, and hands. Such an incorrect perception almost guarantees that you will throw the shoulders and arms, and with them the club, outside the swing plane you took the club back on; for the average golfer, this move almost ensures a weak, sliced shot. Again, keeping a continuous counterclockwise turning of the hips going will eliminate any feeling that you need to hit with your upper body.

Third, and I think most important, the reason you must keep your hips actively clearing to the left is that you will be able to give your hands and arms the needed space to fully release through impact.

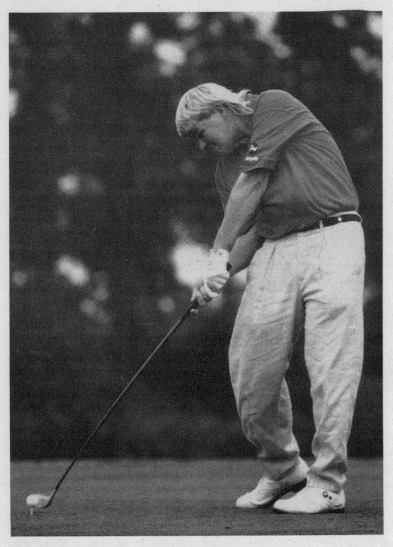

Clearing *your hips allows you to approach the ball correctly from inside the target line and release your hands, arms, and the club more freely.*

Take a close look at the accompanying photograph of me coming into the ball. Can you see how my arms and hands approach the ball from inside the target line, yet my hands have plenty of room to work past my body? When you're in this position, your hands can make a complete release, and a complete release is necessary for you to square up the club at impact.

Many golfers who have the capability to give the ball a good ride cheat themselves out of power because they don't make a good circular hip turn on the downswing. Instead, they make too much of a hard lateral hip slide toward the target. Instead of turning the left hip to the left, they drive it laterally well beyond the point it occupied at address. This feels like a powerful move, but the fact is, if the left hip doesn't clear, then the lower body blocks the hands from releasing the club at impact. The hands can't release the clubhead so that it moves as it should, from inside the target line prior to impact, onto the target line at impact, and then back to inside the target line after impact. Instead, the arms, hands, and clubhead approach the ball from inside the line, but instead of squaring up and then moving back to the inside, the hands (and with them the clubhead) are forced to continue to move from the inside out. So the clubhead path through the ball will start the ball to the right of the target.

Another flaw that the exaggerated lateral hip slide creates is that, in addition to the altered swing path, the clubface itself will remain open to the target line at impact. The reason? The clubface will naturally square itself to the target line at a point when it's the same relationship to your body that it was in at address. If your left hip and side are, say, six inches to the left of where they were at address, then the clubface will not square up until it, too, is about six inches beyond the point where it was sitting squarely at address. The clubface can't catch up to the lateral drive and is still open when the ball is struck.

So you see, a lateral hip slide is a prime cause of push-sliced shot. Not only does the ball finish far right of the target, but because the clubface is also open in relation to the path of the swing the hit isn't square. So you therefore lose distance as well as direction.

I can't emphasize too much the importance of making contact while the clubhead path is precisely on the target line, with the clubface pointing directly at the target. You have to hit the ball absolutely flush to maximize both your distance and direction. And to ensure that you can hit the ball flush, you have to give your hands plenty of room in order to release and square up that club.

If you read a lot of golf instruction you may have the impression that most poor shots are a result of releasing the arms and hands too early so that power and accurate clubface delivery are lost. Actually, I think the opposite is true. Too many golfers don't release the club at all. Or at least, not at the instant of impact when it's needed. And I think a lot of it has to do with the fact that so many golfers slide rather than turn their hips through the downswing. It's not like they're saying, "I don't want to release the club so that I hit it long and straight." It's just that they're putting themselves in a position so far ahead of the ball that they can't release the arms, hands, and club the way they want to.

This is why the old image of "turning in a barrel" has really stood the test of time. It helps you transmit the power from your lower body into your upper body and finally the club, while at the same time keeping you in position to release the club freely through the impact zone.

Remember what I said earlier about the golf swing being one continuous turn. Just as you should turn to the maximum to the right on the backswing, you must keep turning to the left as much as you can while coming down. As long as you're making a circular turn rather than a sway toward the target, you'll be in great shape at impact.

HEAD BEHIND BALL FOR POWER

In your address position with the longer clubs, although your weight distribution between the feet is fifty-fifty, most of your weight will be behind the ball because, if you recall, the ball should be positioned virtually opposite your left hell. So if you drew a line straight up from the ball, your entire upper body, including your head, would be positioned behind the ball.

Now, if you can turn your lower body properly through the downswing, it should be easier for you to do what I want you to do with your head – which is nothing. Maintaining a head position behind the ball through impact is a key to powerful shotmaking – I'll explain why in a moment. For now I just want you to understand that having a relatively still head throughout the swing will allow you to be much more consistent in your shotmaking. I don't want you to make a stiff, tight swing by trying to keep your head in a vice, so to speak. Instead, I think it's easy to see that if you keep turning around a fixed centre throughout the backswing and downswing, you head will stay pretty still. However, if you're driving your lower body at the target on the downswing, it's pretty hard to keep your head behind the ball. It will almost be forced to move forward with your hips, resulting in that lack of release that I mentioned earlier and mishit shots in general.

That aside, here's why maintaining that head position behind the ball will be a big help in maximizing your power off the tee: Doing so automatically helps you sweep the ball of the tee slightly on the upswing. And when you do that, the ball will carry and roll substantially further than it would if you were to hit with a descending blow. The reason? When you hit down on the ball you impart backspin on it. Therefore, the ball starts off flying fairly low but then rises or "upshoots" later in its flight. Logically, it will then drop to the ground at a steep angle and won't roll far after landing. Conversely, when you sweep the ball, contacting it just as the club is moving upward, very little backspin is applied to the ball. Consequently, it zooms off the clubface and flies on a more even parabola, so that it lands at a shallower angle and rolls farther.

If you have been hitting down on your tee shots, you'll add at least twenty yards to your shots by simply staying behind the ball on the downswing and hitting the ball on the upswing.

This super flight pattern with the driver is a direct result of keeping your head and upper body behind the ball at impact. Remember that the lowest point in your swing will always be opposite the centre of gravity of your body. When you centre of gravity stays behind the position of the golf ball, the lowest point in your swing will automatically be behind the ball as well. You won't have to make any particular effort to scoop at the ball to hit it on the upswing, but rather, it will happen naturally. (Incidentally, this is also why you may have noticed that the extra-long hitters usually tee the ball up pretty high with the driver. They stay behind the ball very well and contact it a little more on the upswing, making the hit as flush as possible to the loft angle of the clubface.)

So you see, everything works together in producing a powerful and accurate delivery of the clubface to the ball. You hit the ball a little on the upswing because you've kept your head and upper body behind it. You've been able to keep your head behind the ball because you made a nice full circular hip turn on the downswing rather than driving the hips laterally toward the target. That powerful unwinding action of the hips was triggered by the key first move of the downswing – slamming the left heel back on to the turf.

USE YOUR ARMS AND HANDS

After you clear your hips, there's only one other thing I'd like you to keep in mind regarding the downswing: Feel free to go ahead and rip the club into the ball with your arms and hands.

Again, if you've read or watched a lot of golf instruction, you've probably heard that the hands and arms should remain passive through the impact zone. The reasoning is that if you've done everything right to this point, the centrifugal force you've built up will carry your hands and arms through the shot with no further effort from you.

Now, I've disagreed pretty strongly with a number of pieces of swing advice that you've heard previously. On this one, I'm also going to disagree, but not as strongly. It's true that if you've built up leverage through all the steps we've discussed, to a great degree your hands and arms will be carried along for the ride. They more or less have to hit the ball; they couldn't just stop of their own accord before impact.

However, I don't agree that you should be passive with your hands and arms through impact, for two reasons. First, as I've suggested earlier, I don't believe most club players are guilty of releasing the club too early from the top. Particularly among medium- to-low handicap amateurs, the more dominant fault is not getting a good free arm and hand release through impact. Second, I believe that given the proper sequence of motion and the build up of power through the sequence, you will build more clubhead speed by actively utilizing each link in that chain, rather than by assuming that the link will work fully without your making it happen.

If that last sentence sounds as though I mean you should consciously rip the clubhead through impact with your forearms and hands, yes, that's exactly what I mean. Until just before impact, you've been pretty much passive with your hands and arms since starting the club away from the ball. You've used your body, not your hands to generate tremendous force up to this point. Now it's time to make that last link in the power chain work for you. To me, really whipping the club into the ball with my hands and wrists is a real treat. Don't be lazy at the bottom of the downswing. Go ahead and rip right through it with a full release of your hands and wrists.

I might add here that you should take this aggressive approach through impact on all your full shots, not just with the driver. I believe you should keep the full-swing principles the same for every club in the bag, unless you're in a situation in which the circumstances definitely call for a special type of shot.

But I really don't like to vary my swing pattern too much because consistency is really the name of this game. And in terms of shotmaking, you'll find that using my power swing will help you hit the ball much higher as well as longer than you ever have before. Hitting higher iron shots is an immediate benefit because it will allow you to drop the ball closer to the flag even when it's in a tight position.

THE FOLLOW-THROUGH: FULL AND BALANCED

Take a close look at the photographs (overleaf) of my swing, which show face-on and side views of my finish with the driver. One thing I think you'll immediately notice is that, although I might have just sent the ball away on a 350-yard flight, I'm in an extremely balanced and relaxed-looking position. There is no sense that any flailing, leaping, sliding, or any other unnatural moves that would affect good balance have occurred during the swing. You can't fake a good finish; a balanced end-of-the-swing position can only be a postscript to a swing that was totally in balance.

When you complete the swing, take inventory of your position. Start by checking your left leg; it should be in a relatively upright, firm position with just a touch of flex in the knee. The left leg can only be upright in the finish if it stayed relatively straight rather than bowing out during the downswing. This firm left leg at the finish indicates that the hips have made a nice counterclockwise turn throughout the downswing, as opposed to the hard lateral drive that makes you feel like you're generating power but ultimately leads to poor balance and mishit shots.

Your weight at the finish should be planted almost completely on the heel of your left foot as the result of the full unwinding action of the hips. Just a tiny amount of weight should remain on your right toe, since your right foot has been pulled up and around by the force of the downswing hip turn.

Ideally your chest should be pointing to the left of the target. That's another result of a powerful downswing turn. As with the length of the backswing, how far the upper body turns into the finish will vary from individual to individual. You probably won't be able to turn into the finish as far as I do, and that's okay. It would be great if you can at least end up with you chest pointing directly at the target. This would indicate that you've made a full and vigorous body turn through the ball.

As with developing the fullest possible backswing as discussed in Chapter 2, the benefits of working out with a weighted club will show themselves in a fuller follow-through and finish as well. Slow, controlled swings with a substantially weighted club will help you gain extension through the ball and then gradually extend onto a fuller finish position. Just as the extra weight in the head and shaft will actually stretch your shoulders, torso, and hips to turn in the finish, at least to the point where your upper body faces the target.

In my swing, the hands finish behind the head. My hands are still loose and relaxed on the grip, so that the clubshaft extends around and almost faces the target. Your finish probably won't wrap the club so far around you. The clubhead will likely be handing down more behind you than winding back in front of you. Again, that's okay as long as you've let your hands go as far as they can.

As a final thought on the downswing, I'd just like to encourage you by saying that as you work on the elements I've

Above and opposite: My relaxed finish proves that I made an on-balance power swing.

outlined, and also use the weighted club to improve your flexibility, you will develop a motion that is much more graceful, flowing, and powerful. And of course, you'll see a whole different kind of golf shot coming off your clubface, too. That's the point of all the efforts you are making. Trust me when I say that you will have to practice your new technique diligently, but the gains in direction, distance, and scoring will be worth it to you many times over.

DALY'S DOGMA

Plant Your Left Foot

In order for the downswing to be a perfectly timed chain reaction, you must replant your left heel as soon as you reach the top of the backswing. This is an unorthodox movement of the body, but doing the following drill daily will make it feel like second nature.

Stand on your right leg only and swing the club to the top. Pause for a split second. Next, replant your left foot on the ground, heel first, and then swing the club down. Finish the swing on your left foot only.

Give It a Belt

Because I stress the importance of replanting the left heel and clearing the left hip on the downswing, I don't want you to get the impression that the right side plays a passive role in the golf swing. On the contrary, once your left side triggers the downswing, it's the right side that must rotate briskly through the hit zone for your clubface to powerfully compress the ball.

To promote a good release, try to finish with your belt buckle or belly button facing the target.

Practice with a Broom

Leg drive on the downswing is probably the most overrated element of a good golf swing. In almost every pro/am I play in, I see evidence of this. The typical club golfer makes a good backswing, then drives his legs laterally toward the target. This lunge of the legs hinders the release of the hands-arms-club unit in the hitting area which causes the clubface to be open at impact. The result: a slice.

A drill that will force you to release the club properly with your hands is to swing ten times daily with a broom.

Cure for Your Hook

If your problem is hitting drives that fly on a severe right-to-left hook pattern, the clubface is definitely closing at impact. However, your swing may not be the root cause. It could be that one of the following two problems with your equipment is the root cause of your hook:

1. The grips on your clubs could be too thin, which means you'll exaggerate wrist action in the hitting area and close the clubface.

2. The shafts on your clubs could be too flexible, which means that the head of the club is flexing too far forward and closing the clubface in the impact zone.

Cure for Your Slice

If you're delivering the club into impact with an open face and hitting a slice with the driver, you might want to check with your local pro to see if your equipment is properly suited to your natural strengths and tendencies:

The shafts on your clubs might be too stiff for you, which means you lack the strength and clubhead speed to whip the clubface squarely into the ball.

The grips on your clubs might be too thick, which inhibits the releasing action of your hands and causes the clubface to be open at impact.

Using a One-Iron

A one-iron is one of the most useful driving clubs made. Actually it features more loft than the average one-wood, yet I bet if you polled golfers around the world, the one-iron would be their least favourite club.

In the past, I think amateur golfers were justified in fearing the one-iron; the old designs featured such a narrow clubface that even the pros called it the "knife".

94

Today, however, the one-iron features a large head and is sole weighted. Therefore, it is aesthetically more pleasing to the eye and easier to hit. My advice: If you don't have a one-iron, buy one that looks pleasing to your eye and feels good, because it will allow you to hit more narrow fairways and will thus save you vital strokes on the course.

Once you purchase a one-iron, go to the practice tee and do this drill: Tee up a dozen balls and hit six of them with a seven-iron if that's your favourite club. The put the one-iron in your hand and pretend it is a seven-iron. Swing at the remaining six balls and prove to yourself that your problem was mostly in your head.

Clear the Way for the Club
In making the transition from the backswing to the downswing, many club-level golfers make the mistake of pulling the driver down hard with their hands. Pulling the club down is okay when playing a short iron from rough. But since a tee shot demands that you hit with a sweeping action, you must create a shallow angle of attack by rotating your hips to your left at the start of the downswing. This clearing action of the hips allows your arms to swing away from your body and whip the club powerfully through the ball.

High Tee
When hitting a driver, the club should contact the ball on the upswing. To encourage the necessary "uppercut" at impact, pretend that there is a second ball teed up extra high about an inch in front of the ball you are about to hit. Knock that forward ball off its perch and watch the one you hit sail into the sunset.

12 GOLF BALLS
FREE

WORTH £22 WHEN YOU SUBSCRIBE TO **GOLF MONTHLY**

...AND SAVE UP TO **15%** ON THE REGULAR PRICE OF A SUBSCRIPTION

Keep in the swing with every issue of Golf Monthly throughout the year and receive 12 top quality golf balls – absolutely FREE!
What's more, if you subscribe for 2 years we'll also give you a <u>15% discount</u> on the regular price of a subscription – that's a saving of £9.60!

A Golf Monthly subscription will ensure you receive every issue, *delivered direct to your home*, at no extra cost. It's just one of many valuable subscription benefits:
● Be first in line to receive all free gifts offered with the magazine.
● Be first with all the playing tips, important tournament news and reviews in every issue.
● Receive FREE postage and packing – worth £8 a year.
● Beat any increases in cover price that may occur during the period of your subscription.
● You'll never miss an issue.

Tick Your Choice

☐ SAVE 15% on a 2 year subscription – pay only £54.40 instead of £64, a saving of £9.60! PLUS 12 FREE GOLF BALLS.

☐ Annual subscription for only £32.00. PLUS 12 FREE GOLF BALLS.

MONEY-BACK GUARANTEE

The unused portion of your subscription will be refunded without question if at any time you are not totally satisfied with Golf Monthly.

Send orders to: Golf Monthly, FREEPOST CY1061, Haywards Heath, West Sussex, RH16 3ZA.

Or call our CREDIT CARD HOTLINE on
0622 721555